Successful Strategies for Improving Counseling Programs

Alice Healy Sesno

ROWMAN & LITTLEFIELD EDUCATION

A division of
ROWMAN & LITTLEFIELD PUBLISHERS, INC.
Lanham • New York • Toronto • Plymouth, UK

Published by Rowman & Littlefield Education
A division of Rowman & Littlefield Publishers, Inc.
A wholly owned subsidiary of The Rowman & Littlefield Publishing Group, Inc.
4501 Forbes Boulevard, Suite 200, Lanham, Maryland 20706
http://www.rowmaneducation.com

Estover Road, Plymouth PL6 7PY, United Kingdom

Copyright © 2011 by Alice Healy Sesno

All rights reserved. No part of this book may be reproduced in any form or by any electronic or mechanical means, including information storage and retrieval systems, without written permission from the publisher, except by a reviewer who may quote passages in a review.

British Library Cataloguing in Publication Information Available

Library of Congress Cataloging-in-Publication Data

Sesno, Alice Healy.
  Successful strategies for improving counseling programs / Alice Healy Sesno.
      p. cm.
  Includes bibliographical references and index.
  ISBN 978-1-61048-372-8 (cloth : alk. paper) — ISBN 978-1-61048-373-5 (pbk. : alk. paper) — ISBN 978-1-61048-374-2 (ebook)
  1. Educational counseling. I. Title.
  LB1027.5.S4267 2011
  371.4'22—dc23
                        2011030323

*To my wonderful husband, Frank
and
my beloved sister, Mitzi*

Contents

Preface		xi
Acknowledgments		xiii
Introduction		1
To the Counselor		3

Setting Up—Establishing Routines   5

1	Know Who You Are!	7
2	Manage Your Boss	8
3	Meet Your Colleagues	9
4	Set Up a Professional Office	10
5	Become a Master Planner	11
6	Get Your Plan Approved	12
7	Meet Your Constituencies	13
8	Maintain a Working Schedule	14
9	Create a Network of Advocates	15
10	Understand the Budgeting Process	16
11	Maintain a Log of Activities/Results	17
12	Master the Memo	18
13	Speak Effectively with Others	19
14	Plan Ahead for the Help You Need (Finding a Mentor)	20

15	Build Your Program, Step One	21
16	Build Your Program, Step Two	22

Ongoing Activities—Programs for the Now 25

17	Maintain a "Suicide Watch"	27
18	Beat the Bullies! Maintain Gang Awareness	28
19	Self-Esteem Is a Success Secret	29
20	Provide Career-Building Experiences	30
21	Become Your Teachers' Ally	31
22	Keep Teachers Involved!	32
23	Dress for Success—and Rapport!	33
24	Consider Outreach Services	34
25	Cover Your Assets!	35
26	Maintain Your Morale	36
27	Master the Interviewing Process	37
28	Learn Psychological First Aid	39
29	Confront Cheating	40
30	Interrupt Academic Self-Destruction	41
31	Prepare Kids for Relocation	42
32	Develop Peer-Mentoring Skills	43
33	Build Social Skills among Students	44
34	Encourage Stress Reduction	45
35	Develop Threat-Assessment Awareness	46
36	Overcome Personal Depression and Despair	47
37	Work with Parents!	48
38	Promote Financial Fitness	49
39	Nourish Thinking Skills	50
40	Understand the Power of Culture	51
41	Master Listening!	52
42	Understand Discipline!	53
43	Recognize Generational Values	54
44	Promote Joy and Happiness	55
45	Confront Child Abuse!	56
46	Incorporate Ethics into Your Professional Activities	57
47	Support Beginning Teachers	58
48	Speak Well and Convincingly	59
49	Maintain High Expectations	60
50	Know How to Say Goodbye	61

Contents   vii

The Great Counselor Questionnaire   63

Selected Bibliography for Counselors   65

To the Principal   67

The Principal's Role   69

    51 Participate Early in the Hiring Process   71
    52 Use the Interview as a Launching Pad   72
    53 Use Staff Meetings as an Inclusionary Tool   73
    54 Have a Formal First Meeting   74
    55 Do Your Homework (Office, Mission Statement)   76
    56 Schedule Counseling Staff Development Meetings for the Entire Staff   77
    57 Have a Counselor as Part of Your Advisory Team   78
    58 Share Information   79
    59 Express Approval of Counselor's Area of Expertise   80
    60 Spend Some Time in Their Office   82
    61 Invite a Counselor to Sit in on Selected Conferences with Parents   83
    62 Be as Involved as You Can Be   84
    63 Share Budget Information   85
    64 Take to Administration Meeting(s)   86
    65 Provide Time and Funds for Their Attendance at Professional Development Meetings   87
    66 Support Your Head Counselors   88
    67 Be Aware of Duty Assignments   89
    68 Share Counselor Efforts as Part of the Total School Plan   90
    69 Make the Counselor Aware of Your Goals regarding Counseling   91
    70 Suggest or Join a District or Superintendent's Committee regarding Counseling   92
    71 Request Minutes of Counselor Meetings to Ascertain Needs   93
    72 Provide Cadre of Retired Counselors for Emergency Times   94
    73 Listen   96
    74 Publish   97

75	Support Emotional Intelligence	98
76	Support Bibliotherapy	99
77	Be Sure They're Part of a Team	101
78	Remember to Motivate	102
79	Focus Each Day (The Power of Five)	103
80	Are They Modeling You? (Who Are They Modeling?)	104
81	Highlight Importance of "Mothering" (Promoting Students' Mothers!)	106
82	Have Interim Evaluation/Progress Assessment Meeting(s)	107
83	Be Aware of Occurrences in a Counselor's Personal Life	109
84	"It's Always Been Done That Way" (Support Necessary Changes)	110
85	Clarify Your Motive(s) for Involvement	112
86	Patience	113
87	Integrate Ideas—Take from Academic and Use in Counseling	114
88	Bring in the Stars	115
89	What about Discipline	117
90	Total School Team Interim Evaluation	119
91	Report Successes, Share Success Strategies, Visualize Successes	120
92	Associate with Positive Colleagues	121
93	Have a Success Discussion	122
94	Get Them Off to a Great Start! (The First Day of School)	124
95	Not Always Mr. Nice Guy	125
96	Be Alert to How "Customers" Feel about Them	126
97	What about Crisis Plans, Teams, Situations	127
98	Get Out There	129
99	Maintain Focus/Ask the Right Questions	130
100	Be a Great Manager and Coach	132
101	*Know* You Can Do It and Do It Now	133

The Super Principal's Checklist	135
Selected Bibliography for Principals	137

Appendix A: Sample Grid	139
Appendix B: Log of Guidance Services	141
Appendix C: Numerical Report on Counseling Activities	145
Appendix D: Fog Index	147
Appendix E: Adam and Alice's Magic Tips for Talking to Adults	149

Preface

Counseling programs are alive in our schools today; however, like so many school services, they are often greatly understaffed, and counselors are greatly overworked. Today's counselor is a very well-educated professional with skills on hand to promote the academic and emotional health and well-being of students.

These skills are desperately needed in today's educational climate, but often because of budgetary stringencies counseling programs are faced with severe cutbacks and in some instances, elimination. Rarely does one hear of an expansion of these programs—and yet when major school crises occur, and unfortunately they are occurring with more and more frequency, this particular professional group is called upon to restore normalcy to the school climate in addition to all of their other duties.

With today's focus on education almost entirely on academic achievement, the students' psychological well-being and feelings often take a backseat. While the coping skills for getting along with others and for dealing with the problems of growing up and handling academic demands are more important than ever, the programs and services mainly concerned with these areas are often in jeopardy. This book was written with the hope of reinforcing those programs by offering strategies to counselors and principals that they might use to strengthen existing programs and to lay a firm foundation for expansion.

Most counseling programs are under the radar at this time. An important gem of our school community is not being seen in the light of its true value.

It's time that attention and support be given to this often forgotten asset. In November 2010 the Hope Diamond was placed in a new setting at the National Museum of Natural History in Washington, D.C. Thousands of new and past viewers of this spectacular gem lined up to see it in its new glory. It shall be returned to its original setting in a few months. However, time and steps were taken to remind us that we did indeed once have this marvelous forty-five-carat-plus diamond in our possession.

We in the school community have a similar treasure in school counseling. This book was written with the goal of using the talents and skills of counselors and principals who by working together as professionals can support and enhance this service, thereby supporting and enhancing the entire school community. It is hoped that the strategies and activities presented herein will go a long way toward achieving that goal.

Acknowledgments

Much thanks to all the counselors and principals whose comments and suggestions made this book possible.

Special thanks also to William Aston, Lana Brody, Carol Fox, Dorothy Gram, John Hall, Frank Kwan, Chie Masumoto, Judy Oberlander, Julie San Miguel, Marla Shwarts, the staff of the Palos Verdes, California, library, and Winfred Strong.

Very special thanks and much gratitude to the highly skilled Lori Trent and the multitalented Dr. Woodrow Sears.

Introduction

This book was organized in two separate sections: one for counselors and one for school principals/administrators.

The counselor section contains suggested activities and strategies especially structured to meet the needs of the school counselor (kindergarten to twelfth grade). Both new and experienced counselors may find these suggestions helpful as they seek to renew, refine, refurbish, and/or restructure the counseling programs at their schools. A bibliography, questionnaire, and selected attachments are also provided.

The second section focuses on the ways and means by which the school principal can help develop, monitor, maintain, and enhance the counseling program at his or her school. In addition to the various strategies presented, there is also a specific bibliography geared to the principal's managerial needs as well as a Principal's Checklist for enhancing counseling programs.

Counselors may wish to use this book as a reminder of successful school counseling practices they might have forgotten or a possible introduction to new ones they might wish to incorporate into their existing programs. The Counselor's Questionnaire provides counselors with a way of looking at themselves and their programs that might trigger greater effectiveness, while the bibliography and various attachments offer ways and means by which programs can be supported and expanded. A review of the principal's section can also afford counselors ideas and topics they might wish to share with principals as they strive together to strengthen and expand the counseling programs.

Principals may wish to use this book as means to provide them with an overall view of a counseling program (counselor's section) and techniques and procedures for greater personal involvement (principal's section). The Principal's Checklist is a way of self-assessing this issue, while the bibliography is a good starting point for further exploration in the managerial realm.

Principal and counselor professional groups at the school and district level may find this book quite helpful as a discussion guide. In addition, professional counseling organizations might wish to use this as a reference guide to successful counseling practices and ways of encouraging administrative support.

Professors in graduate schools of education concerned with counseling and school administration programs might wish to use this as a supplementary text for their students, helping them gain practical insights into everyday program development and management.

To the Counselor

Counseling services for students should be available from the elementary grades forward. Students should know their counselors and how to access their services. As our society becomes more complex, more of us use the services of helping professionals. Learning how to access such services—school counselors in this case—is an important part of the preparation for life.

The disadvantages of not knowing how to take advantage of counseling support show up most vividly in high school, where general-track students receive far fewer counseling services than do students on the academic track. As a result, many general-track students do not benefit from the variety of courses open to them, and their access to postsecondary educational opportunities is often compromised.

Consider this: Perhaps many general-track students could have entered the academic track or had more satisfying school experiences had they received early and continuing support from professional counselors.

This section was written for *professional counselors*, educators whose academic preparation is based on a body of knowledge rooted in guiding individuals toward achievements and successes they might otherwise miss. The operant word here is *professional*, and the strategies offered in this book were crafted from my own rich career and interviews with hundreds of school counselors across America. All strategies offered can be used without asking permission (although it is wise to have your principal as a partner), all require some degree of personal discipline, and all will enhance your reputation as a competent, caring *professional*!

Using the strategies listed will allow you to demonstrate your skills and knowledge-based competence that are the hallmarks of counseling professionals. The young people you influence and other educational professionals you support need now, more than ever, the insights and sensitivities your training has provided. I am pleased you chose this book to take your professional preparation to another level of readiness to serve, support, coach, and counsel students and their teachers.

SETTING UP—
ESTABLISHING ROUTINES

Setting Up—Establishing Routines

Savvy Strategy 1: Know Who You Are!

A story from World War II: Actor Kirk Douglas, driving from Los Angeles to Palm Springs, stopped to pick up a hitchhiking soldier. Surprised to see who the driver was, the soldier exclaimed, "Do you know who you are?"

This Strategy concerns confirming and reinforcing your sense of self in your role as a professional counselor. Whether you are a seasoned counselor with many years behind you or new to the profession with your career in front of you, your sense of self matters.

This Strategy calls for a new daily regimen. Specifically, begin every day with a quiet moment to set yourself into your role. You might say, "I am a professional counselor. I am not a teacher, nor the principal. I am not the custodian, nor anyone's parent. I am not anyone's friend. I am a professional counselor with skills to assist young people in making choices and finding the strength to have a meaningful and successful school life. This is what I do. This is the person I will be today."

Follow this affirmation with one or several success targets for the day, such as: I will help Paul control his temper. I will help Mrs. Jones and David repair their relationship. I will be accepted by all I meet today as a professional. AND, visualize these things happening! The *Wall Street Journal* reported several years ago that a private school counselor in New York visualized every student being accepted by a college—and it happened.

You see athletes "pumping up" before taking the field, and you hear of champions visualizing the course and seeing themselves winning. A San

Francisco surgeon confessed that a major reason for his good reputation was beginning each day visualizing scheduled procedures being completed successfully. Should you not give yourself the same competitive edge? Can't you "see" Paul winning over his anger, and Maria being accepted at Hobart? Do it. Take responsibility for your success as a professional counselor!

At the end of the day, record your successes. What a powerful way to set yourself up to win tomorrow! This system works. Too many people have proved that "when you believe it, you will see it!" Make it work for you!

Motto: *Knowing who you are sets the tone for all you do!*

Savvy Strategy 2: Manage Your Boss

California consultant Christopher Hegarty wrote a book, *How to Manage Your Boss*. In it, he lays out strategies for understanding your boss's concerns, pressures, priorities, and biases, and he instructs you in using that knowledge to present yourself and your programs in ways that will allow your boss to say Yes!

Your boss may be the principal, an assistant principal, or some other administrator. Regardless of the title, that person needs to know you are on his/her side in meeting objectives, achieving results that have been promised, or supporting personal agendas that may be well outside school goals. This Strategy truly is essential to your success!

Schedule a meeting early in the school year, whether you are a new or returning counselor. Prepare for the meeting by obtaining copies of current goals, objectives, or rules of the school. Study them and be prepared to demonstrate your knowledge of them. In particular, the objectives of your counseling program should mesh with those of the school.

However, one of the purposes of the meeting is to give your manager an opportunity to suggest ways your program might be modified to be more supportive of his/hers. Therefore, it will be seen as a courtesy to give the boss a copy of your program plans a day in advance so he/she can be prepared to talk with you about the details of your plan. This demonstrates good headwork!

Specifically, you want answers to these questions: (1) Is what I propose to do what you want/expect? (2) Does my planning document meet your requirements? (3) What changes would you like? (4) When can we meet during the year to discuss progress, achievements, special problems, and opportunities? Again, good headwork and a supportive attitude are demonstrated by asking to receive feedback. (You will find yourself to be the exception among the staff!)

What format should you use? Ask the school secretary for the correct format. Provide outline-level details, with specific targets for meeting with teachers, students, and parents. Also, include letters you plan to write and other documents for which you will ask his/her approval. This is the information that identifies you as a collaborative staff member—and, frankly, one who can be managed while accepting responsibility and taking initiative. A winner!

Motto: *Little goes forward without the principal's push!*

Savvy Strategy 3: Meet Your Colleagues

A school staff is a large and complex social system, organized around the concept of providing educational services for students. Each member has a role to fill that affects the performance of the entire school. All are your colleagues, with information to share and with influence on the students whom are your primary clients. Accordingly, it is important that you meet each staff member. Realistically, they cannot work with you if they do not know who you are!

Begin with the school's table of organization (T/O). See how the school is organized—how many nonteaching professionals and support staff are listed. Make sure everyone is on your copy of the T/O—and make sure your name and function is listed, too. (If not, add your name in the appropriate place, make copies of that page of the T/O, and give it to people as you meet them.)

Also, you need to know the names of key staff in the district office, the school board members, and all of those who volunteer in support of programs at your school. The list can be quite long, including: custodians, cafeteria staff, office staff, principal and assistants, nurse, psychologist, social worker, various aides, parent organization officers, and other individuals who provide support services to students (sponsors of clubs, etc.).

When meeting people, get current telephone numbers and e-mail addresses—and make certain each knows how to reach you! (If the school does not provide you with business cards, create your own and use them—with student clients, too.) Then, be sure to keep your T/O current.

Remember, this is your primary network—the source of student referrals and the people you will need to work with to create support systems for students in difficulty. The first step in an intervention often is a call from someone who has seen a student doing/saying something nonconforming. You, the school counselor, are a safe person for people to call when they are unsure about whom to call but they are certain that someone needs the information they have.

As you meet people, make a list of what you learned about them—and add to it as the school year progresses and you see/hear other things. Sometimes, the solution to a student's problem will be found in that list of personalities and interpersonal styles. Obviously, you want to keep this information confidential and locked away from prying eyes.

Motto: *Knowledge is power. Know the power of the staff.*

Savvy Strategy 4: Set Up a Professional Office

Too often, the counselor's office is barely more than a closet—leftover space after all other administrative personnel got offices. Sometimes, intrepid counselors find spaces of their own, often with the help of custodians. Whatever the space, make it comfortable, friendly, and functional. (Notice that in the private sector, "offices" frequently are cubicles. Space management requires planning!)

In small spaces, wall colors and pictures are especially important. (See citation by Schauss in the Bibliography.) A decoration can be a single picture, perhaps by a student, that you can use as an icebreaker: "What do you think of the picture?" Flowers and curtains also contribute to emotional comfort, as does muted background music.

For "tools," you need: a locking file cabinet and file folders; telephone; computer/printer; bookcase and resource manuals; tape recorder and tapes; writing supplies; a card file or electronic equivalent; digital camera; and more—especially age-appropriate materials for young children.

The object is to create a space that is utilitarian but friendly; a work space in which the client is the center of attention, in which the counselor and counselee can face one another to confront curriculum planning or other personal growth possibilities. Ideally, that means a seating arrangement with a desk against the wall so you can turn to it to write but that does not create a barrier between you and the counselee.

Also, it is important that counselees are convinced of the confidentiality of the information they share and how the "counseling process" works. Thus, as in a dental or physician's office (where payment requirements are described), it is useful to explain the function of the *office—the role of the counselor*—during the first minutes the counselee is in the office. You might also have a descriptive brochure available. Parents, especially, find this helpful.

As always, personal tastes and styles will influence office décor, but all choices should reflect attention to a single criterion: Will this support the counselee in feeling comfortable in working with me so that our mutual task can be completed successfully? It is surprising how many items can be distracting or disturbing. Posters that are aggressive or authoritarian in tone (i.e., "My way or the highway!") are clearly inappropriate.

Maintain a log that chronicles the daily activities and plans for tomorrow and keep it locked while you are out of the office. It may prove to be your most valuable tool.

Motto: *Create an oasis of calm in a sea of chaos.*

Savvy Strategy 5: Become a Master Planner

A friend who worked in Slovakia found a disturbing saying there: "If you want to hear God laugh, make a plan!" Nevertheless, all good work begins with a plan, continues by plan, and is refined in the future by learning from the plan what worked, what didn't, and what was overlooked. Planning is a powerful tool!

To make it easier, here is an acronym you can use—SOLER—in which:

S   stands for Survey, gathering all resource materials needed;
O   stands for Organize, putting materials in order to be used;
L   stands for Launch, putting the plan into action;
E   stands for Evaluate, checking the validity of the plan's elements; and
R   stands for Revise, correcting your plan based on evaluation feedback.

Another saying in common use is "The devil is in the details." Truly, the higher the level of detail at which you plan, the more likely you are to identify the details that would have caused you trouble. This is important because planning is simple. There are only three ways elements in a plan can connect. One, some things must happen before others can. Two, some things cannot happen until others have ended. Three, some things can go on at the same time.

This is true whether you are developing a plan to increase reading comprehension among third-graders or planning to refuel a nuclear power plant. Write your plan's elements on 3" × 5" cards, and lay them out on a desktop. Follow the logic above and you will see what needs to be done, with whom, and when. Then tape the cards on flip-chart paper, and your plan has assumed a visual form.

Also, this format allows you to show your plan to others and to get them to help you make corrections (moving/adding cards), and if you add up costs to be incurred on each card, you will have created a "quick and dirty" budget.

This is another example of "a picture is worth a thousand words," especially when you want to get the attention of a busy administrator. Be prepared to get a quick approval from someone who will appreciate your good headwork and homework!

This approach to planning is called the "precedence method," and it is covered in greater detail in most contemporary texts on planning or project management (another powerful skill for you to consider). When you demonstrate your thinking in these effective ways, your potential for contributing becomes more fully recognized. That, probably, will lead to other important professional benefits!

Motto: *A master performer always operates from a plan!*

Savvy Strategy 6: Get Your Plan Approved

Out in the private sector, this would be called "selling your plan." Wherever you work, a plan that is not approved is not going to be supported. Consequently, you must present your plan to your supervising administrator before your year's work is going to pay off for students and be rewarding for you. *Your* is the operant word, because your plan will substantially define you as a professional.

First, one plan presented in narrative style will be very much like another, so find out what format your supervisor prefers and adapt your plan to it.

Second, if you used the planning technique presented in Strategy 5, your major tasks have been defined, the resources you need will be obvious, and the people (students, teachers, other staff) who will be involved can be identified.

Third, spell out the educational/behavioral objectives of each program element so they meet the TAM criteria—tangible, achievable, measurable. When results can't be measured, they can't be proved (and probably didn't happen).

Fourth, explain how results will be measured (pretest/post-test, interviews, observations, anecdotal reports from teachers, etc.). Be sure to use a variety of measurement techniques and, when possible, involve others as assessors (so the results you report are validated by other competent professionals).

Fifth, present a plan that is challenging, but rational; that is, you will have to work diligently, but the work you propose to do can be done in the time you have.

Even though it's two decades old, a useful article by Podemski to retrieve is "Psychological Contracting for the Counselor's Role: Procedures for Counselors and Principals." It highlights the important issues and expectations to come out of such meetings, and it emphasizes the old concept of the "psychological contract," in which trust is established.

Nothing creates a better basis for trust than a plan that is competently developed and effectively presented and lays out tracks that can followed. Your plan must meet your manager's expectations but provide as well a basis for inspections so your works-in-progress can be monitored. This will be a real test of your professionalism and of the potential value of your services.

Motto: *Well begun is half done!*

Savvy Strategy 7: Meet Your Constituencies

Your nominal clients are students but, realistically, you will be working with a broad range of people on the school scene. None are unimportant—even that parent, long absent from a child's life, who arrives on the scene wanting to be involved, can become the "parent from hell" in a matter of hours. Unless . . . when he/she meets you there is recognition that you are a professional who offers—and demands—respect from everyone with whom you interact. "Yes," you say confidently and with a strong handshake and an unwavering eye, "I am your son's counselor. How can I assist you?" Strength. Structure. Poise. Assertive. Tough.

Tough? Why not, as a backup position. Counseling, ultimately, is about assisting students and others to make choices—in taking tests, in choosing courses, in personal behavior. This requires clarity of purpose without moral ambiguity and an abundance of ability to be as firm and demanding as required.

Wow! How do you put all that in a letter to students, to their parents? How do you communicate that when meeting other faculty members or when being introduced at a PTA meeting? Choose positive, strong action verbs. I believe . . ., I expect . . ., I will support . . ., You will find me to be . . ., I want to accomplish . . . .

Do you plan to *write* to students and parents? Then a draft of the letters you plan to send should have been attached to your plan for your manager's review. Do you plan to use any forms, short notes, or other documents that are not already in use in the school? Attach those, too, for your manager's review.

Will you be introduced in formal assemblies? civic clubs? churches? Then why not ask for a *few minutes* to do a PowerPoint presentation that can project the *umph!* of your program better than a short talk.

And speaking of talking, learn to *project* your voice. No one should ever have to struggle to hear what you are saying! Even small people can speak with authority and be heard by persons sitting at the back of the auditorium. Present yourself as a person for whom *best outcomes for kids* is your major purpose in life. Let them meet someone they want to know better.

The days of friendly, but indifferent, counseling are over. In the past, too many counselors shortchanged students by being unprepared and uncaring, more concerned with discipline than with academic performance and providing life-coping skills. Everyone remembers those counselors. Now, let them meet you!

Motto: *Getting to know you is more than just a song!*

Savvy Strategy 8: Maintain a Working Schedule

Most schools run on a defined and predictable schedule. Some say only prisons have more rigid schedules. Students live by their schedules. Teachers, too. And counselors must as well.

When are you available? When are you unavailable? When you are not in your office, where are you? All this information should be posted on your office door, and your supervisor should have a copy, too, in case you are needed to respond to an emergency. The freedom from tight routines carries with it the responsibility to be a disciplined performer—and a role model for counselees.

On your office door, or on a board near it, you should post your weekly schedule. A brief note should tell students how to make an appointment. A standard form should confirm the student's appointment and what documents (if any) must be brought to the meeting. The model you want to emulate? A very busy professional services office (e.g., medical, legal). (See Appendix A.)

Time management is an important skill. That does not mean depriving yourself of coffee and lunch breaks, but it does mean making sure you are performing and producing results at a level that is beyond criticism.

The truth about professional services—and doctors, dentists, lawyers, and psychologists all know this—is that cost-effective/profitable operations come only with the ability to optimize, if not maximize, the time spent with clients each working day.

While school counseling is not a profit-making operation, it can be proven to be a highly cost-effective service. That proof begins with numbers—students seen, results obtained, parent meetings, etc.—and the numbers grow in relation to your accessibility during and after school hours. And, realistically, all good results begin with clients being able to schedule time with you.

Remember, most kids will avoid anything associated with hassles. When students report to their peers that meeting with you is easy and satisfying, the demand for your services will increase. That's when your administrator will notice you and when your status among faculty and staff will increase. As simple as it sounds, all that can begin with a schedule and contact procedures posted on your office door. Make it work for you! That's why a sample schedule grid is given in Appendix A. Why reinvent the wheel?

Motto: *Let them know where you go—and when!*

Savvy Strategy 9: Create a Network of Advocates

Maybe you haven't thought of them that way, but advisory groups become advocates for you and your programs—if you manage them well. Nothing gets an administrator's attention more than a flurry of phone calls, faxes, and e-mails from parents, community leaders, and even students. In real life, a dozen phone calls about a single issue means a newspaper or TV reporter cannot be far behind.

Schools are a community's property and, often, its largest expense. Consequently, every community is full of people who want to give advice on school operations. The best way for people to get involved is through advisory groups.

It is within the charter of most in the counseling profession to organize advisory groups—of students, teachers, parents, community/business leaders, other educators, and even groups of people associated loosely as "Friends of Ambrose High School." If you work with them to develop agendas your school administrators approve, they can be powerful allies in selling your program and getting community resources for your students. Remember, *approved agendas*!

Meetings: Never longer than an hour or more than once a month. Always an agenda, circulated in advance. Make sure reports are *brief*, with copies for everyone. *Advisory* means offering recommendations, not giving orders, so the *tone and content of recommendations* must be crafted with approval in mind. Even in school board meetings, make sure your advocates *speak for* your program and not *against other programs or individuals*.

Do NOT involve negative individuals in advisory groups—get people to serve who want you and your program to succeed, and steer clear of those who want to push an alternative or opposing agenda. That is best done by having *someone else chair your advisory groups*. Your role is to do the staff work (including soft drinks and snacks) and to make members look good and feel appreciated. There are hundreds of books on organizing effective committees. Read some. Take courses in small group management. Become an expert!

Always be sensitive to the fact that you are a school district employee, and you must not embarrass your administrators by being quoted or taking actions that are not fully in concert with district policies. That will only take energy away from your program and compromise your ability to be an advocate for your students.

Motto: *You are not alone—but pick your friends carefully!*

Savvy Strategy 10: Understand the Budgeting Process

All institutions, public and private, are driven by budgets, and they are limited, too. If no funds are allocated to support a program, hire clerical support, or fund community activities, those things cannot happen—unless alternative sources of money can be found (reread Strategy 9). Your success as a *counseling program manager* will depend, in some part, on your understanding of, and contributions to, your school's budgeting process. You already know that when costs must be cut, counseling programs are, historically, among the most vulnerable.

The first and greatest commandment is this: Know how to prove that you and your program create value in excess of your salary, benefits, and operating costs. That means you must find out how to assign monetary value to improving attendance, reducing vandalism and violence, and increasing students' ability to score well on achievement tests. Any negative act prevented is a cost saving!

To operate effectively, there are things you need that the district (or someone) must pay for: telephone and postal expenses; visits to other campuses or district meetings; attendance at seminars and professional memberships; books, journals, and periodicals; computers and programs; hiring speakers or renting/purchasing special-topic (i.e., terrorism) videos and materials; and funds to assist students with special needs or legitimate emergencies.

Many administrators still do not encourage or permit staff to participate in the budget-development process. Be proactive. Find out when the budgeting process starts, and be prepared to be the first staff member with a *defensible* budget request for the following year. Ask for a brief meeting to go over your budget with your administrator. (Maybe someone on an advisory committee could help you get ready for that meeting. How wise you would be to get that help!) It will be another way to demonstrate your competence and professionalism.

Guess what? Counseling is not the only special program in the educational community. Every year, there seems to be another government-mandated program to be included in local curricula. Each has a constituency, both in-school staff and citizen supporters. You must be prepared to do combat with them, and other special pleaders, for always-limited funds. Know how to convert your "facts" into numbers that demonstrate value (See the sample chart in Appendix B). Remember, education is big business!

Motto: *A carefully prepared budget is a mark of professionalism.*

Savvy Strategy 11: Maintain a Log of Activities/Results

Budgets and other program projections are always based on current operations or recent history in other schools. In the same way that most people will forget to record out-of-pocket expenses for reimbursement, even professionals frequently forget to keep a log of activities and achievements. Then, when confronted with the question "What did you achieve this year?," they cannot respond promptly with a catalog of achievements and thus miss an opportunity to sell themselves and their program and to highlight noteworthy achievements.

This Strategy is to alert you to the need to always be able to respond to the question, "So, what have you done for me lately?" You can do that most easily by keeping a tally each day of students seen, meetings attended, letters written, parents contacted, presentations made, and counseling cases closed. *Every day!*

Create a form that is easy for you to use. Keep it in sight, on the wall next to your desk or under a transparent cover on your desk. Provide space for the annotation of noteworthy details. The proof—if not the devil—is in the details!

But why wait to be asked about your results? Why not provide a monthly tally of your activities and results to your administrator and appropriate others (such as chairpersons of advisory committees, program advisors in the district office)? This is NOT about bragging but about *proving that you are "earning your keep"* and creating value every day! (See Appendix C.)

There is a continuing movement toward "performance management" in public schools that will result in removing school staff who do not meet standards or negotiated expectations. When that time comes, everyone will have to know how to keep tallies and to turn routine activities into measurable performance criteria. What a powerful way for a school counselor to make friends and allies among the faculty than to be able to master these skills!

Understand, *this is a skill!* Often, really mediocre performers achieve star status in school systems because they know to tell their stories, to turn ordinary activities into wow! experiences, and to give their administrators stories to tell at district meetings. When real numbers are used, however, those inflated stories will be discounted and the *real performers* will be recognized. In the meantime, why not consider that your administrators will appreciate your contributions?

Motto: *Watch the numbers—and see how they add up!*

Savvy Strategy 12: Master the Memo

Many advise never putting anything into writing if it can be avoided. Once words are sent on paper, they get a life of their own and are hard to recall or disown. Since some messages must be conveyed in writing, then learn how to do it like a professional! Begin by mastering the memorandum (memo).

Memos can be one line ("Can we meet Friday at noon for lunch?"), but usually they are longer. Three paragraphs should be the outside limit. For longer communiqués, write a report of a page or more and send it forward with a short covering memo; for example, "Please see the attached trip report and list of expenses."

Why three paragraphs? The first allows you to "frame" the subject; the second allows you to add details; and the third allows you to ask for or to propose action. Use another format for anything more. An example:

> During a recent meeting with Mrs. Roberts, the parent of Jasmine Roberts, grade 5, I reminded Mrs. Roberts of the importance of having Jasmine's records from Millwood School forwarded to us. She said that she had stopped at Millwood and they said the records were being sent. She had obtained a signed note to that effect from the school secretary last week.
>
> I called the secretary to ask for the records and she said, ". . . all in due time." This has happened twice in the past with Millwood.
>
> Perhaps you could use your good office to contact Millwood in order to expedite this situation. Millwood does not have a school counselor.

To say more than this would be unnecessary and abusive to the recipient—as though he/she is somehow culpable. If this short memo does not initiate action, neither would a longer message. Short memos reflect an ability to *think and to convey information effectively.*

Maybe this format seems familiar. It should. It is the suggested discipline of the Internet. Use e-mail for short messages and, when necessary, use the "attachment" utility for longer messages. That way, you don't keep the telephone line tied up while you compose (a cost!), and for most people, it is more "natural" to write and edit reports off-line, using a familiar word processor.

Then, there is the fact that a "paper trail" often is necessary to protect yourself. Short memos with an official date/time stamp become powerful defensive weapons when required. Without them, you need a lucky charm! Be sure you select easily understood words for your memo. We recommend using the Fog Index (Appendix D) to check. It's fun and tells us a lot about how we communicate.

Motto: *When meaning matters, use a masterful memo!*

Savvy Strategy 13: Speak Effectively with Others

Most of our communicating is done one-to-one, and it is distressing to notice how many people lack the understanding of the effective use of this basic tool. This Strategy is not about "common sense" but rather about thoughtful talking, as though the recipient is as important as your message. Otherwise, your message may get lost in the larger message of insensitivity to the person you want to reach.

Insensitivity? Use my name. Do not talk down to me, either by your tone and choice of words or by standing while I am sitting. Do not make me feel inferior by using threats—I know our roles and relative positions.

These simple rules are especially important when talking with students, but they are powerful, too, with those you want to influence. Suppose you want to "connect" with Jane, who is sitting with a cup of coffee in the teachers' lounge. You pull up a chair and sit, so you are at the same level, and maybe (be sensitive to culture here) you touch her arm and say, "Jane, I can't tell you how much I appreciated your support of my presentation at the meeting last week. As a new counselor, your vote of confidence in my program was like a big hug from a friend. Thank you!" Your message over, you can stand and leave.

Unless you speak to someone on his or her level, eye to eye, the opportunity to convey intimacy or sincerity is minimized. Likewise, speak only loud enough to be heard by the person you're addressing, and keep your language—choice of words—professional! Too many people sacrifice their effectiveness by trying to emulate the street language of some students. Real professionals—physicians, dentists, attorneys—don't make that mistake. Neither should counselors.

Eye contact is important in conveying a personal message. So is facial expression. Both, along with the choice of words and the message, make the recipient feel to be at the center of your universe for a few minutes—a very special feeling indeed. If there are "secrets" to communicating, these are a few of them.

Students want to know that you care; so do their parents. Use words that express positive expectations and the possibility of success. Smile and project the image that you are at ease, comfortable in the situation, maybe even that you like the person(s) you're with. Allow people to leave you feeling good about themselves, and you will have given them a gift of immeasurable value.

Motto: *Speak wisely and well to touch the people who need to hear you!*

Savvy Strategy 14: Plan Ahead for the Help You Need (Finding a Mentor)

One of the hallmarks of maturity (as you may tell your student clients) is knowing when to ask for help. The same is true for counselors. There will be students whom you cannot help out of your own resources, and that is when you need to have a trusted colleague to whom you can turn. Maybe it is someone you consider a mentor, a former professor or a senior counselor whose experience and wisdom you have learned to trust. Know how and when to "refer out." Keep a phone list of community resources.

One wise and experienced counselor in Ojai, California, said, "You have to know your limits. For example, if you've had a recent death or suicide in your family or circle of friends, that may not be a time when you can listen attentively to someone who is incapacitated by grief." It is a mark of professional maturity to be able to say, first to yourself, "I cannot handle this right now," and then to refer the client to someone else while you call that trusted friend or mentor for help.

But sometimes, you need that friendly helper when you are just plain "stuck"—when you have a student with whom you cannot achieve a breakthrough, when nothing in your experience or training is working for you. How comforting it is to know that you can call on a Mary, Sam, or Dr. X to ask for help!

Finding a mentor is not always easy. Perhaps the most difficult part of that process is admitting your need for continuing support and being available to receive it. Colleagues in the teachers' lounge usually are inappropriate mentors, for all the obvious reasons. That means you have to reach outside your circle—and perhaps your "comfort zone"—to find your special resource person. When you do, you will have to ask for that person's support because competent people rarely volunteer to give away more of themselves. But being willing to ask for help in advance is a good sign of serious professionalism. It probably means that you are a person who will pass that help along—in kind—to others. Mentors generally are continuing what someone started with them years before—a chain of goodwill, reaching those who will never know where it all began. Your university counseling professors could be excellent mentors. Try them.

Maybe the best way to find a mentor is to be one yourself, investing in the growth of others for no reason other than that it's the right thing to do. Sadly, these are gifts that not everyone gives, and worse, they are not given because the need to do so is not a part of their character. There are takers, not givers, even among counselors.

Motto: *Ask for help, give help, start a chain reaction!*

Savvy Strategy 15: Build Your Program, Step One

All the strategic suggestions in this book really are about building your school's counseling program, but this Strategy and the next focus on things school counselors can do *by themselves* to build strong programs. This Strategy is oriented toward building your program *within the school.*

First, even if your program is not new, you must communicate the way it supports school goals—to teachers and other school staff, to parents, to students. The easiest way is by announcement letters distributed to students and staff and mailed to parents. But these letters must be short and specific—no more than one page—and shorter is better. No one will read a two-page letter! (Preliminary copies should be approved by the administrator.)

Your letters should specify the school's goals and your complementary program goals. They should spell out (1) the types of student issues to be dealt with; (2) the numbers of students to be seen each month; (3) the numbers of presentations to be made during the semester; (4) the types of information to be provided. And you should include a possible "helpful hints" newsletter three or four times throughout the school year.

Make sure your role and your program are shown on the school's table of organization; that you negotiate with your administrator several opportunities to speak about the program at staff meetings or as in-service training; that you make new materials available to staff on request (do not distribute materials people do not ask for!); and that you offer short presentations or briefings to assist teachers with special class modules. (This is an easy way to become known as willing to be helpful to teachers—if your presentations are well received by students.)

Smart counselors submit *frequent* reports of achievements to the administration, listing numbers of students seen, issues dealt with, and problems resolved. Administrators like to have this kind of information available as "filler" to use in district meetings to highlight staff achievements. One way to improve on raw numbers is to issue "chits" to students who receive counseling services and on which they can write comments. The student gets the original; the counselor keeps the copy. That way, names, dates, issues, and comments are recorded.

You can pick up other ideas at district meetings of counselors and from the literature. The important thing is to tell constituents what you will do and provide data that prove you are doing what you promised. That builds credibility!

Motto: *Tell your story, and illustrate it with facts!*

Savvy Strategy 16: Build Your Program, Step Two

The last Strategy was about *having a story to tell*. This Strategy is about telling that story to the public beyond the school's parents. How do you do that? It's called publicity and relationship building with people who can tell others about your school and its counseling program. (How many civic clubs in your area invite people to make presentations? Could you do twenty crisp minutes on counseling?)

Why is counseling important? What *measurable* results are you obtaining among your students and faculty? Does your district have a person responsible for public relations? If so, you need to meet that person who is the pipeline of school news to the media. If there is no such role, then you need to build your own relationship with media representatives. (TV and radio stations must devote a percentage of air time to community and public service programming, and they need stories!)

All media will report on "giant snake found in local elementary school." But will they report reductions in absenteeism and vandalism? Yes! Will they report on improved math and reading scores? Yes! Here's how *you* do it:

Improvements can be proved only by measurement—so measure everything you do. Build a database that describes academic performance in your school, and report improvements. This is important information in community newspapers. Be creative and get your school and your program on TV!

One counselor held a Christmas Open House in the counseling office where walls and tabletops were covered with student achievements as the payoff of counseling services. Parents came. So did media representatives—because he invited them! Another counselor invited the school district's state legislative representative, who was a magnet for media reps, to attend counselor-sponsored events. (Involve your administrators. No principal wants to meet an unannounced reporter and a TV cameraman! Make sure your administrators get good press.)

If you get visitors to come, give them something to do. Involve them in brief dialogue sessions with students. Let them take student achievement tests. Show them letters from local businesses and lists of student achievers. Make a visual display of counseling services and numbers of students participating.

Send them away with program descriptions, *and your business card.* Look like a professional! More than anything, the media respond to people who help them get good stories. Of course, you have obtained your administrator's permission for all this involvement.

Motto: *The most exciting stories are based on results. Tell about yours!*

ONGOING ACTIVITIES—PROGRAMS FOR THE NOW

Ongoing Activities— Programs for the Now

Savvy Strategy 17: Maintain a "Suicide Watch"

There is no doubt that pressures on students have never been greater—pressures to perform academically, to conform to peer group norms (both positive and negative), and to cope with the economic and social pressures of single-parent homes. Nearly every school-age child in America knows at least one student whose home life is wretched, whose personal conduct is self-destructive, and who is in desperate need of support from a caring adult.

Adolescent suicide is a major health problem, ranking two or three as the cause of death in most jurisdictions. The causes of suicide and its avoidance are being studied in many medical centers, but there is a single finding that serves as a common denominator: The most important step in suicide prevention is early detection so that remedial treatments can be taken.

For many adolescents, the school counselor may be the most likely professional to make that first significant intervention that saves a young life. Why? Because counselors are trained observers of young people. Counselors usually have networks of students and teachers who report behavior changes and comments among students that signal personal despair.

I was a team member in developing a curriculum titled Suicide Prevention in California Public Schools. It presents to senior high school students a methodology for coping with fellow students who might share suicidal feelings. The four-session curriculum focuses on the importance of (1) listening; (2) being honest; (3) sharing feelings; and (4) getting help. It stresses the importance of NOT keeping certain kinds of secrets. (There are also single-session modules designed for presentation to teachers and parents.)

Many communities already have suicide-prevention programs and hotlines. This is a built-in opportunity for professional counselors to tap into local resources and perhaps to become a resource. Bringing in outside professionals for briefings to teachers and groups of parents will add to the counselor's credibility. (Even if you say exactly the same thing, using the same words, there are some who will not hear you the way they will listen to Dr. So and So from the Community Health Center.) In addition to the information referenced above, there is information in the public domain that will allow you to build an effective antisuicide program.

Motto: *Intervening to prevent a suicide is a gift to humanity!*

Savvy Strategy 18: Beat the Bullies! Maintain Gang Awareness

Part of life in groups is learning how to deal with bullies. On the playground, older children terrorize the smaller ones, physically and emotionally. In upper grades, the bullying may take more adult forms of intimidation that will be seen throughout postschool life. It is an important part of the socialization process to teach young people how to deal with bullies and to teach bullies more effective ways to relate to other students.

In this period of dynamic destabilization, it is important not to forget that teachers, too, often find themselves to be the victims of bullies. With the approval of your administrators, why not develop and present programs for both students and teachers, something like "Coping with Bullies in Four Easy Steps"? Be up to date on cyberbullying. Have a desk copy of *Cyberbullying* by Sheri Bauman.

Yes, there are resources available! One of the most user-friendly is the small book, *Jake Drake: Bully Buster.* Author Andrew Clements has crafted a text for children—or to be read to children by their parents—that explains what bullying is and how to deal with it. One place this book is required reading is The College School (grades one through eight), on the campus of the University of Delaware. The College School has established the elimination of bullying as one of its priorities.

Dealing with the issue of bullies allows counselors to put other antisocial behaviors into perspective. Sexual harassment is a form of bullying, as are most forms of racial discrimination. Allowing students to see bullying as just one face of abuse of power and role is important. When the opportunities for individuals to participate is limited by abusive others, democratic processes cannot operate. When counselors create and present such short courses, they provide great lessons in democracy and problem solving that can be used throughout life.

Once you begin to see the counselor's role as that of an educational specialist in solving life problems, a wide world of opportunities to inform and to serve opens up. Why not a two- or three-session course on anger management? What about stress management? The possibilities are almost without limit when you look at the entire spectrum of dealing with bullying.

In addition, maintaining gang awareness is important here. Gangs have many bullying aspects, and a liaison with police departments is especially vital. Dealing with gangs must be done in conjunction with the many agencies set up just for that purpose. Know who they are and use them if necessary. You can't handle this one alone.

Motto: *Defeat bullies and build democracy in the classroom and life.*

Savvy Strategy 19: Self-Esteem Is a Success Secret

Positive self-esteem is absolutely essential for success anywhere in life. It is the certain knowledge that one is worthy of succeeding, is deserving of friends, and is able to face life each day with positive expectations. These personal attributes are to be found among all who contribute—in the professions, in sports, in communities, in business. In the simplest terms, self-esteem is feeling good about oneself and the freedom to go into any venture or enterprise with the expectation of succeeding. It is so important. . . .

But so many students suffer from low self-esteem, coming from years of marginal grades, lack of familial support, limited financial resources, patterns of exclusion from "in-groups," and association with others whose lives are similar. To be sure, counselors can do little or nothing about all those life circumstances, but counselors can provide young people with a variety of coping skills that will teach them to turn life's lemons into lemonade!

One really powerful resource you can use to learn about confidence building and self-esteem is the classic reference, *100 Ways to Enhance Self-Esteem in the Classroom* by Jack Canfield and Harold Clive Wells. Another is *Character Builders*, a K–6 series by Michele Borba. With resources such as these, you can create powerful programs for students—and for faculty, staff, and parents, too!

One of the best teaching aids is someone to model desired behaviors—and counselor, you can be that role model! A little extra effort, a lot of planning, and a willingness to share your resources will identify you as one of the special people who make life better for others. That is citizenship in action, and that is a large part of what being a role model is.

One almost immediate payoff from self-esteem training is that it encourages individuals to become more *personally and socially responsible*. People with high self-esteem do not leave their trash for others to pick up. Neither do they forget to do the things they promised—from homework to club assignments to chores at home.

These are the behaviors that underlie good citizenship and community building. The people who exhibit these behaviors tend to be those who get selected for leadership roles and also are active in contributing to the success of others. Every school needs more of them! Counselors often become actively involved in developing school programs to improve self-esteem and personal and social responsibility. In doing so, be sure you obtain administrative approval for this and any other program inclusion.

Motto: *Self-esteem is a prerequisite for all good deeds!*

Savvy Strategy 20: Provide Career-Building Experiences

Self-esteem and acceptance of responsibility are two enormously important attributes that employers look for. Once you have these characteristics programmed into your students, then it is time to give them work experience in real work settings. Part-time work, internships, part of the formal school curriculum (with or without compensation), or individuals working for small or large businesses over the summer and other school holidays—all are invaluable.

Some schools, such as Woodland High School in Hartsdale, New York, have instituted formal internships for the second half of the senior year. It's called the WISE program—Wise Individualized Student Experience. Students "go to work" in local industries to learn firsthand what life at work really is like. The school's administrators and teachers found it cured "senioritis," that special lethargy that comes when seniors know they will graduate and college admissions have been granted. "Going to work" puts life back into the final semester.

Unless your school has a formalized program, the counselor's role may be limited to calling local industries and asking if they are willing to provide work and learning opportunities for students. If so, then students need to learn the basics of a job search, interviews, and workplace discipline. (It is surprising how many students have no work experiences and no knowledge of how people get jobs.)

High school work experiences can be life shaping. One senior investment broker admits that it was a part-time job in high school, answering phones and getting coffee for brokers, that was the origin of his love for the stock market. Likewise, many young women are attracted to medical careers after serving as "candy stripers" in hospitals while in high school. Such experiences give students a sense of wholeness in connecting the relationship between their studies and the requirements of the jobs they observe or fill.

Let's face it: Counseling is becoming increasingly important as "good" jobs with opportunities for advancement become fewer and more jobs are based on services and offer limited tenure. Those who identify career direction early, and direct their studies to support applications to targeted industries, are the ones who have the greatest opportunities for personal and career satisfaction. Effective counseling is a major gift of the school to its students.

Motto: *You found your career—now help them find theirs!*

Savvy Strategy 21: Become Your Teachers' Ally

Schools exist for students and teachers. A principal is necessary; so is a secretary. Everyone else is optional. Teachers know this. Too many "supplementary staff"—including some counselors—do not figure this out, thinking themselves to be more important than teachers. Some always take the side of the parents, students, and administrators against teachers. Teachers know this, too. For you to succeed, you must convince the teachers that you are there to assist them in coping with difficult students and to support the school's academic program.

"How can I help you?" is a good question to ask every time you meet a teacher. If your help is desired, the next question should be, "When will it be convenient for us to meet?" Then, you juggle schedules until a time is found that suits the teacher. Message: "I am here to support you. You come first." When you talk about the student(s), a good opening question is, "What do you think the problem is?" Another is, "How do you think I can best help you?"

This line of questioning affirms the teacher's role as the key person in the student-teacher-counselor triangle. If you do not believe this is THE fact—and act on it—you will have a difficult time. Yes, even good teachers can be wrong, and there are a number of teachers who should not be in the system. Still, you must get the teachers on your side, earn their trust and support, or they will undermine you! How? Hundreds of ways. Make sure you don't have to learn the hard way!

Perhaps you can offer help to them personally. You might suggest to your administrator that you be allowed to provide a college counseling service to requesting teachers. Some commercial businesses today offer school/college counseling services as part of a total benefits package to employees. These employees can then use the services of a licensed school counselor to assist them in selecting private schools at the elementary and high school levels that would be appropriate for their children.

Services are also offered to employees seeking guidance in the selection of colleges for their children and tips on available scholarships. What a terrific service to offer to teachers, and what a fabulous way to become and obtain an ally!

Remember, teachers are survivors! They have survived bad classes and good, bad principals and good, students who were unteachable and students who could not be kept entertained. They need an ally. They will repay with support.

Motto: *Do everything possible to make the teachers' lives easier!*

Savvy Strategy 22: Keep Teachers Involved!

In addition to being the teachers' ally, you will have greater success working with students if you keep their teachers informed and involved with the regimen you want to implement. Ask the teacher to be your partner in devising a success plan for the student(s) involved. This honors the teacher's investment in the student and lets the student know that the teacher and counselor are a team and cannot be manipulated to be opponents. (Clever students can do this!)

In worst-case scenarios, teachers want the student expelled from class. When this happens, the counselor must become a negotiator. Here are some points to consider:

1. Recognize that the student is difficult.
2. Agree on a trial period to develop/implement a remedial plan.
3. Agree to take the student out of class at times the teacher accepts (within reason).
4. Schedule a conference with the student's parents/guardians.
5. Allow the teacher the option of participating (in point 4).
6. Commit to a regular schedule of meetings with the teacher.
7. Provide written reports on your view of the student's progress.

Remember, most public schools get money based on numbers of students in attendance each day. Therefore, "kicking kids out of school" is not an option. Here are some guidelines for working with teachers in more reasonable situations:

1. Meet teachers when it is most convenient for them.
2. Clarify teacher expectations. (A "fix" is impossible in one meeting!)
3. Provide feedback on progress while maintaining confidentiality.
4. Present the guidance curriculum in class if the teacher wishes.
5. Assist teachers in interpreting "trouble signals" in papers or behavior.
6. Empower teachers by building their coping and problem-solving skills.
7. Provide checklists to assist teachers in logging changes in dress, personal hygiene, grades, friends, mood, and attendance.
8. Always be courteous, professional, caring, and kind.

Most teachers have developed coping skills and strategies, but most will appreciate tips and guidelines you can provide—through staff development training sessions or working with individual teachers and their students. Telling success stories—anecdotal reports from other classes/schools/studies—usually is an effective way to provide information without appearing to be teaching or lecturing. Use questions such as, "Have you tried . . .?" or "What about trying . . .?" or "What do you think will work with . . .?" This keeps the teacher in a peer/colleague role!

Motto: *Be sensitive to teachers' needs and feelings—and win with them!*

Savvy Strategy 23: Dress for Success—and Rapport!

Counselor clothing communicates. So does the setting in which counseling is done. Both matter in having maximum impact on students, both in their attention and their responses. Many counselors feel that more formal (rather than less formal) dress and settings enhance student acceptance of information.

Experiment! Match your attire to your goals, and see how the students respond. When you talk about interviewing for jobs or colleges, conservative attire (suit, white blouse or shirt and tie) would model the appropriate behavior. When you talk about collaboration and team building among students, upscale casual attire (pressed slacks, shirt/blouse, and a cardigan sweater) would suggest how student leaders might want to dress for success. When do you wear jeans? Never—except for special camping, hiking, cooking, and cleaning events. Another clue—don't wear to school what you would wear to the beach.

What is the dress code for your school? If you cannot tell by looking, ask! Be sure you don't get trapped by "The Hidden Dress Code Dilemma," as discussed in the article by Robert M. Lang (Clearing House, 1986). Dressing in the manner of your supervising administrator is recommended as a way of staying above criticism. Expectations are not always stated! But it is difficult to classify someone as a professional who's wearing flip-flops, cutoffs, or tank tops.

Since dress is a behavior, make sure your choice of attire or style does not distract the students with whom you work. Women should know the rules—even young male students can be distracted by "sexy" attire. But beyond revealing clothes (men, too!), pay attention to jewelry, hairstyles, glasses that are twirled rather than worn, and overdoses of perfume/cologne.

Alas, it is necessary to mention personal hygiene—not just body odor or soiled garments, but clean hands and neatly trimmed nails. Pass this test every day: Would I want my child to be counseled by someone who looks, dresses, and acts the way I do?

One dress rule that travelers learn is that with a blue blazer, pressed slacks, and polished loafers, you can go anywhere. Maybe that fits schools, too.

Remember, students respond to the total package—how you look, speak, smell, and present yourself. Don't let a favorite bracelet or a persistent habit of scratching your nose or scalp limit your professional acceptance. Your training and intelligence will carry the day, so don't let the cosmetics get in your way!

Motto: *Package yourself for effectiveness—all the pros do it!*

Savvy Strategy 24: Consider Outreach Services

Beyond the public relations benefits you may receive, there are a number of outreach kinds of things counselors can do to provide important services. Since you have expertise in dealing with school-age children, why not share it? One familiar format for doing that is the occasional newsletter. Another is making presentations at parent-teacher meetings, civic clubs, and in newspaper columns.

Nearly everyone is concerned with how kids think today, and why? Adults want to know about trends in delinquency and ways to reverse them. What adult really knows how to communicate with kids? More important, perhaps, is how to help children talk to adults (see Appendix E, Alice and Adam). How do you develop conversational skills? These are things you know about, both as "how-to" information and readings and from other sources that adults can access.

If you are launching a suicide prevention/awareness program, this is a topic nearly everyone finds interesting. What are the "danger signals" to look and listen for? What are the myths about suicide that block interventions and prevention?

Teenage alcoholism? Always a hot topic. "Success Tips for Single Parents" could make you a regular presenter in the Parents without Partners network. One counselor organized a successful presentation around the issue of Christmas gifts. It was titled, "Don't Overspend!," and it emphasized alternatives to high-dollar gifts that can build stronger parent-child relationships. These are things people want to know about! And you, counselor, can do this—and more!

Yes, your primary responsibilities are to the school, its teachers, and its programs. You serve these by enabling students to enhance their performance and to cope with the pressures in their lives. Your professional preparation and your experience with students give you a lot of information you can share—as a community service and as a goodwill builder for your school. In many areas, school counseling is without public support—because people don't know what a strong counseling program can contribute to students and the community at large. If you make the effort to reach out, it will be appreciated—and rewarded!

A last suggestion: A New Year letter (no religious conflicts!) about resolutions and setting them with students to create a focus on achievement and skill building. What parent would not appreciate such information?

Motto: *Reach out to contribute, and watch the positive returns come to you!*

Savvy Strategy 25: Cover Your Assets!

You probably know this as CYA, and it means the same thing. Few people in the school community are more at risk for criticism, misunderstanding, misquoting, and litigation than counselors. Why? So much of their work involves unhappy people and unhappy information. While the outcome of counseling should be acceptance of personal responsibility, for many, blaming others (counselors!) is preferable to accepting responsibility for their decisions and actions.

Many defensive tactics are rooted in common sense; others must be based on local circumstances. But all of them derive from being aware—all the time—of doing things or being in places that make you subject to being criticized. Like so many professionals, you are held to a higher standard. Accept that responsibility.

Do not go to bars, nightclubs, or "party" in your home community or anywhere you may be recognized by students or their parents. Unfair? Probably, but you know the consequences. Do not make yourself a target for gossip.

Stay in your professional role in all contacts with students, parents, and faculty. Maintain professional detachment—do not get emotionally involved with students or their problems. It will blind you to objectivity and make you part of the problem.

Use your office for all meetings with students; never meet in your car, in parks, in public spaces, or in coffee shops. Such meetings will be misinterpreted and questioned.

Be discreet in *all* conversations about students, their parents, your school, and its faculty or administration. What you are heard to say may come back to haunt you! Even if you can prove inaccuracy, your reputation is damaged.

Be scrupulous about maintaining *appropriate* confidentiality (some student information must be reported to authorities). Reveal nothing to anyone. Keep your records accurate, and keep them locked. At all times! Prevent snooping. Check out FERPA—Family Educational Rights and Privacy Act of 1974.

Do not have "off the record" conversations that have led many counselors to hear themselves quoted in court. "Off the record" offers no protection!

Stay current with your field and the law. The National Board of Certified Counselors recommends at least one hundred hours of professional courses every five years.

Understand requirements for graduation. Make sure no student fails to graduate because you miscalculated points and requirements. Be careful!!

Motto: *Always behave the way you would expect of your physician!*

Savvy Strategy 26: Maintain Your Morale

One of a counselor's unique requirements is that of showing people who have received lemons how to make lemonade— how to see positively when difficult things have happened. That is very much harder to do when the counselor's own life view is pretty bleak. Admittedly, it is more difficult to maintain a positive outlook on those days when everyone you see has or is a problem!

Maintaining morale is a personal challenge for counselors. In an unpublished survey of 344 pupil services personnel (including counselors) conducted by the author, the mean for self-rated morale was 6.7 on a scale of 10. Morale ratings were unrelated to age, gender, or position, but trend analysis showed that morale declined with tenure. Sadly, nineteen respondents said high morale was a result of being new in their roles! This needs more study, but there were some certainties:

- Morale jumps when administrators or fellow staff members show support and appreciation; and, in particular,
- Morale improved when compliments were received, especially from principals, and from teachers and other school staff.

For most counselors, these will not be daily events, so what can be done to maintain morale? In group meetings, counselors reported exercising (jogging, aerobics, swimming, rowing, and yoga); dinners with other counselors to discuss cases (no names, of course) and to learn that they were doing okay; and such simple pleasures as clothes shopping, cooking, movies, reading, and visiting with friends.

Beyond these activities that are available to most people, some counselors reported that their morale is boosted and reinforced by foreign travel, river rafting, painting safaris, parachuting, and other outdoor activities that build self-esteem and confidence. When you feel good about yourself, all challenges seem easier to manage. It is no secret that students with self-confidence and high self-esteem perform better, so it is no surprise that the same dynamics work for counselors.

When successful people are interviewed, their success secrets often are revealed in the most simple terms. A famous motorcycle racer said he would sit on a pile of tires and visualize the racecourse. A world-class surgeon admits to beginning each day visualizing the day's surgical procedures. And a California counselor said, "I love the work I do and most of the kids and teachers. My energy is renewed every day, and every day I am rewarded in some small way."

Motto: *Maintain your vision—and your vigil of your morale!*

Savvy Strategy 27: Master the Interviewing Process

All investigative processes—medical, counseling, detective work—depend for input on interviews. This "intake" process is a first step toward making action or program decisions, as in hiring or firing people at work, assessing need or readiness to accept help, and determining the parameters of the interviewee's problem or situation.

It is a skill as full of subtlety and inventiveness as any you can imagine. Interviewing can best be learned by observing live interviews and then discussing the process and how key information was elicited; for example, asking, "How did you know to ask that question? And at that exact moment?"

Obviously, experienced interviewers "see" patterns and clues. A mnemonic, PIESS, may help you learn to see that way, too:

1. Physical appearance/limitations: Short/tall, attractive, scars, a limp, missing/deformed limb, weight, hairstyle, nails, clothing, jewelry, etc.
2. Intellectual attributes: Bright/dull, language skills, grades, goals, etc.
3. Emotional balance: Active/passive/aggressive/angry, mood swings, tears, constant movement, appears fearful, etc.
4. Social skills: Comfortable/uneasy, eye contact, coherent responses, manners, attentiveness, polite/rude, etc.
5. Spiritual/religious references: Church, faith, God, devils, etc.

Obviously, this is a compressed list that you can develop into a checklist that reflects the nature of your interviews with students. Remember, anything a client brings or wears to an interview provides a behavioral clue and is something you can ask about. (Okay, in these "politically correct" times there are questions you cannot ask. Get that list of prohibitions from your principal or school district.)

Notice that effective interviewers frequently ask questions about the relationships among the visual clues and interviewee statements. Example: "If your mother is so strict and proper, how did she react to your tattoo and your matted hair?" Such questions say that you are listening and observing and that you are not going to tolerate superficial input or otherwise waste your time. Students notice that.

When asked why they liked one counselor over another, one group of students said, "They pay attention to us. If they're writing when you come in or while you're talking, they aren't paying attention!" So, if they respect attention, show them the extent to which you're attentive. "You aren't wearing that big ring today. Did you forget it, or have you made some social changes?"

Motto: *People's behavior tells stories. Notice and ask them to tell you!*

Savvy Strategy 28: Learn Psychological First Aid

Karl Slaikeu defines crisis as "a temporary state of upset and disorganization, characterized chiefly by an individual's inability to cope with a particular situation using customary methods of problem solving, and by the potential for a radically positive or negative outcome." Since counselors often are a first line of assistance to young people experiencing a crisis, preparation and forethought are recommended!

Despite the definition, a crisis is NOT a time to get a radically positive outcome, which suggests a major learning experience, but rather a time for the counselor to assist the client to return to previous levels of coping ability. Managing new information may, in fact, put the client on overload!

Many student-aged individuals can be expected to overreact and to use reasons for grief (death of a grandparent, suicide of a student who may not even have been a friend) as a way to play with emotions and to attract attention. Others, though, when deprived of a major source of support, can be terribly frightened and feel abandoned and vulnerable. For these, Slaikeu's three steps are important:

1. Be available, but not intrusive, and offer listening and emotional comfort.
2. If threats of self-harm are expressed, assess the lethality of the statements and be prepared to refer/call in suicide prevention counselors. (It is important not to overvalue your own skills in this kind of situation!)
3. Have in place a current list of support resources, from temporary housing (following a fire) to replacement of clothes, financial support, and alternative schools/day care that may be required.

It is important for the counselor to maintain composure during what may be highly emotional episodes, to stay calm and capable of responding to the student(s) in need. This is another time when professional counselors must assess their skills and emotional resources fairly and accurately and not to overstretch their own limits. It is less likely that this will happen if counselors have anticipated such emergencies and are prepared.

Dealing with grief is a well-documented process, and much literature is available. Developing a list of community resources, and even joining or taking Red Cross first-aid and disaster-relief training will greatly enhance one's own coping skills. Nothing is going to happen in your school that hasn't been studied and hasn't resulted in the publication of remedial initiatives that have been proved effective. Collect some of this case material, study it, discuss it with colleagues, and be prepared to be needed in crises!

Motto: *The Boy Scouts said it first: Be Prepared!*

Savvy Strategy 29: Confront Cheating

An epidemic of cheating is sweeping the nation. Students in anonymous surveys report cheating at the 70 percent level on tests, athletic competitions, and in personal relationships. University of Virginia physics professor Dr. Louis A. Bloomfield developed a computer program to check for plagiarism on essays and found a distressing level of cheating (*60 Minutes*, November 2, 2002). And everyone is aware of fraud and wholesale theft in American (and European!) corporate life, not to mention the marital infidelity of public officials, icons of royalty, and, as always, media stars.

Parents of expelled students complain, "Everyone does it," and it is common knowledge that collegiate athletes often are allowed to meet lower standards than "regular" students. This epidemic did not arise overnight, nor will it be stopped by the concerns of a few teachers and counselors. However, consider this: Is it possible that the schools with reputations for being intolerant of cheating will find their graduates being accepted at more universities or getting better jobs?

What role can counselors fill in this combat with dishonesty? Try these:

1. Be a role model of integrity, being scrupulously honest in dealing with students, parents, administrators, and teachers.
2. Ensure that all students understand what cheating is and how plagiarism is defined; remove all ambiguity about these issues.
3. Keep the topic alive with classroom teachers; lead discussions on how to make cheating more difficult and easier to detect.
4. Discuss with students cheating, competitiveness, and parents' expectations.
5. Talk about concepts such as honor, integrity, and decency to help students develop positive value constructs.

As laudable as they are, honor councils and student governance are weak vehicles for the enforcement of honor codes. Such institutions can only be as strong as the student body's expectations, and that is the point at which counselors, in union with teachers and administrators *and* student leaders, might be able to make an impact and assist in answering the questions, "Who cares?," "Why does it matter?," and "Why should I be the only one . . .?"

Another suggestion seems appropriate here. What about learning groups? Students who are prepared do not have to cheat. What about organizing learning or study groups, with students cooperating in providing answers to probable test questions? That way, students can "collaborate and graduate" with integrity!

Motto: *By all means, be a model of truth telling, honor, and integrity.*

Savvy Strategy 30: Interrupt Academic Self-Destruction

School counselors often are the first to be able to reach young people who, for no apparent reason, "spin out of control" into patterns of behavior that appear self-destructive and certainly antisocial. Generally, counselors have neither the training nor the resources to cope with seriously out-of-control students, but the first step is to intervene, to interrupt self-destructive behavior.

In the business magazine *Forbes*, an article addressed this subject. "When Rich Kids Go Bad" describes the phenomenon of kids who have everything going for them—good health, looks, intelligence, money—but they begin to self-destruct. Early symptoms: grades drop, looks deteriorate, they skip school, steal, leave home, and break all bounds of parental and social discipline. Such behavior changes are noticed first by peers and teachers—and will one or several of them report the students who are acting out to the counselor? With a little luck. . . .

One of the primary rules of psychological first aid is to challenge any marked changes in behavior immediately. Anyone can ask, "Hey, what's going on with you?" But the counselor may be the only one in the school with the training and skill to turn that kind of asking into an ongoing therapeutic process.

Parental conferences are necessary to enlist support in keeping the student in school and in discovering the trigger event(s) causing the behavior. Divorce, parents under financial pressure, death of favored relatives or friends, drugs? You cannot know until you investigate. Group counseling might help, as well as the assigning of a friend as a companion and mentor—the buddy system often works.

This is a good time to have access to a list of resources available to the school and to the student. Specialized psychological services and alternative schools may be parts of the solution, but nothing is more important than early intervention by the school staff and counselor. Given the distance between so many parents and children, someone at school likely will be the first to notice.

Community resources? Alternative schools? Even residential schools are listed by NATSAP (National Association of Therapeutic Schools and Programs). In some cases, the school district may be obliged to pay all or part of the tuition where parental funds are limited. This is important information in determining therapeutic strategies. Why not collect that information and have it available?

Motto: *Even rich kids need help—counseling is a democratic process!*

Savvy Strategy 31: Prepare Kids for Relocation

Few things about childhood stress have been discussed more fully than the effect of moving—leaving friends and familiar surroundings and having to confront a new home and an entirely new social setting. School counselors can be helpful in two ways: First, by providing some personal and parental guidance for children leaving your school; and second, by providing support for new students who must establish themselves in your school. Fortunately, some of the same guidance materials can be used in both instances:

1. Suggest that parents give children information in advance and allow them to become part of the planning process.
2. Give children specific roles and responsibilities in packing/unpacking.
3. Take pictures of the present school and friends who will be left behind.
4. Provide an address book of friends being left behind (or a book in which to record names of new friends). Parents could include picture postcards of the new city to send to friends left behind.
5. Make a record of topics covered in the student's classes to present to teachers in the new school, along with achievement in extracurricular activities/sports/clubs.
6. Develop lists of physicians, dentists, optometrists, etc., so records can be transferred to service providers in the new city.
7. All of this information can be incorporated into a single binder that says on the cover, "My Relocation Book: Contacts, Responsibilities, Photos." (Many moving companies provided additional suggestions.)

Such an inexpensive giveaway can provide structure that allows students to reduce their anxieties by giving them things to do and information to collect and to create a sense of forward motion instead of abrupt endings. When talking with students about these issues, it is important to encourage them to express what they are *feeling*.

Too often, adults tend to get stuck in the cognitive domain and forget the importance of affect, of feelings, fears, despair—all of which usually can be handled once they have been expressed. This is one situation in which giving students permission to express feelings of impotence and anger can be most useful. When the counselor says, "Of course you feel that way! Who wouldn't?," that may free the student to understand the feelings s/he is experiencing are normal, expected, and part of the learning/growing associated with moving on!

Maybe a useful analogy is that this is the kind of help that may once have been provided by a grandparent or elderly neighbor, someone who could take time to listen to a child in distress and turn tears into anticipation. A good use of time!

Motto: *Get them ready—and let them go!*

Savvy Strategy 32: Develop Peer-Mentoring Skills

One of the tenets of guidance and counseling at all age levels is that clients can participate in designing their own learning, and in choosing their solutions. One of the most creative ways to put this belief into practice is to create peer-counseling activities and opportunities. One of the great cosmic truths is that kids hear each other when they cannot hear adults, and vice versa!

"As peer mentoring catches on, more students are getting a little help from a friend!" That was the supportive observation reported in the *APA Monitor*. We know that using a buddy system in early grades improves both grades and attendance.

As students grow older, it is increasingly possible to tap into that bond of mutuality that develops to foster learning and other positive change goals. At the same time, important skills for life are being developed. Such skills are *listening, asking clarifying questions, giving feedback, and offering help and assistance*. In fact, most adults do not know how to do this! What great learning!

Many students show extraordinary improvements in their academic achievements after mentoring younger students in mastering their learning objectives. Also, some students with behavior problems change their conduct after helping younger students.

What is it that operates there? Acceptance of responsibility? Improved self-esteem? Self-confidence? No matter! It is a powerful device (and one that was used to such great advantage in the old days of one-room schoolhouses). Talk about student-centered classrooms and learning!

To institutionalize peer counseling, it is necessary to set up some formal training for those who will be counselors. This does not have to be extensive, but it should give peer counselors (mentors, really) a basic understanding of (1) how to structure a mentoring session; (2) how long should it be; (3) how often should they meet with those they're helping; (4) where to get necessary materials; (5) how to terminate mentoring; and (6) reporting requirements so the school counselor or professional administering the program can be kept informed of progress and when new assignments are possible. This is exciting skills transfer!

These mentoring experiences can be incorporated into study groups designed to help students prepare for SAT and ACT. With many participating and developing answers, learning is accelerated as well as facilitated!

Motto: *Put the "each one teach one" dynamic to work in your school!*

Savvy Strategy 33: Build Social Skills among Students

It's not news that America is becoming, in the words of the media, "an uncivil society," in which rudeness and in-your-face aggression are the norm. What happened to politeness, courtesy, consideration, and neighborliness as the social foundation of American values? That's too large a question for this small book.

Again, school counselors are called on to model these important behaviors and to demonstrate that assertiveness is socially acceptable, that you can be courteous and self-protective at the same time, and that being polite does not make one a wimp.

Verbal abuse and assaults have come from the streets into the schools, creating teaching/learning difficulties in many American classrooms. Too many students and teachers alike accept harsh language as a sign of being "hip." More likely, it is a defense against isolation, anomie, and fear of others.

How does one meet and make friends? How do well-spoken, gentle people meet and greet? How do you push through your own and others' barriers against hurt and disappointment? Social skill development training, of course! It can be done one-on-one, in group sessions, or in a group guidance class (that many teachers appreciate).

A way to begin is to develop lists of what it means to be a friend and what students want from friends. That could be followed by getting students to pair off to discuss some of the concepts. Role plays could follow, focusing on the issues of misunderstandings, missed appointments, and the cooling of affection. A useful background article, titled "Specific Psychotherapies for Childhood and Adolescent Depression" by J. F. Curry, appeared in *Biological Psychiatry* in June 2001 that deals with the necessity of allowing students to explore such feelings.

When possible, parents should be involved in such training, and they should be given some guidelines that have proved useful; for example, modeling friendship, kindness, caring, sportsmanship, and avoiding negative comments about others.

Games involving parents should avoid the harsh win-lose environment and emphasize instead fun, camaraderie, and maybe a little learning. (One father admitted that his need to win was so compulsive that he couldn't even let his twelve-year-old son win at checkers! He was embarrassed to see life lessons he was conveying to his son, who, just like the father, was having trouble making friends.)

If you haven't read the legendary book *How to Win Friends and Influence People*, get a copy (paperback). It may be the best social skills book in print!

Motto: *To make a friend, be a friend!*

Savvy Strategy 34: Encourage Stress Reduction

A professor returned from five years in Japan thirty years ago, talking about how academic stress was affecting elementary school children, who worried about competing to get into the "right" high school as the path to the "right" university and the "right" life. It seemed comical then, but now something similar has hit the United States. Performance anxiety is stressing out elementary kids. And older ones, too. Again, it is too large a topic for this small book, but stress reduction deserves a place.

No less an authority than the *New York Times* reported that seven Bay Area, California, schools have introduced "yoga breaks" into their school days. A yoga master offered free training to teachers, and the training is being offered in physical education as well as in regular classrooms. The program introduces the physical disciplines of yoga and omits the metaphysical aspects. Results of that experiment have been so popular that it has been replicated in schools in Los Angeles, Seattle, New York . . . and Chamberlain, South Dakota!

Obviously, administrators and parents must be involved in providing this kind of innovation as part of the curriculum. But maybe this is yet another role the school counselor can fill—becoming the conduit through which these kinds of ideas can be brought into schools. Societal demands, changing value constructs, polished advertising, and more are making children's attention spans shorter and shorter. That makes the teacher's job doubly difficult, as does the fact that media exposure is making children aware of a larger universe of things to be frightened of and stressed by.

Even elementary students come up with disturbing arrays of fears and anxieties. One technique for dealing with these worries is to write each "trouble" on tiny notes, insert them into balloons that are then filled with helium, and let them float away. As they watch the balloons disappear, children are asked to shake their hands, roll their shoulders, and let their worries fall away. Shaking and moving in synchronized movements can wake sluggish bodies, as can certain eye and facial movements awake sleepy minds. When kids worry about guns and death, yoga and other stress relievers can be soothing and healing antidotes.

Motto: *Relax! The peak is in sight!* *(Unknown mountain climber)*

Savvy Strategy 35: Develop Threat-Assessment Awareness

In addition to all the other stressors that impact schools, now there is the Office of Homeland Security to warn of threat assessments across the nation. There has been nothing like this in America since World War II.

In 1997, the state of California included the requirement of a comprehensive safety plan for all school districts. But this was more than just another administrative burden. It was imposed to deal with the real and persistent threats represented by gangs, ethnic tensions and fights, off-campus antisocial behavior by students, suicidal or dangerous associations with weapons, and paranoid groups within the community.

Metal detectors and armed police may be on campus to ensure students' safety, but they are constant reminders to students and faculty alike that "evil forces" are a threat to the school. Schools are now routinely required to develop lists of threats, and often counselors are asked to supervise the listing process.

Threat assessment has been defined by Kris Mohandie as "the process of assessing risks to a particular target, individual, or group of individuals and designing and implementing intervention and management strategies to reduce that risk or threat." Therefore, counselors need to comprehend this ugly issue to assume the leadership role they may be required to fill.

All police departments and many universities have programs that can assist schools and school districts in developing threat assessment and security plans.

Further, much work already has been done by many local, state, and federal agencies that can be borrowed or adapted. But one of the main reasons for getting local assessments developed is to raise these issues in the consciousness of faculty, staff, and students. They must be sensitized to threat so they will recognize events and individuals if they appear, and know what to do.

One thing counselors might consider is reading and leading discussions on the very powerful text, *School Violence Threat Management: A Practical Guide to Educators, Law Enforcement, and Mental Health Professionals* by Kris Mohandie. With this comprehensive resource as a guide, you will be prepared to lead a group or to participate in developing threat reduction and management plans for your school. Truly, this is an area of responsibility few imagined—but it's not really new. Threats have always been with us. The ability to address and handle them can be a counselor's gift to students and staff.

Motto: *Forewarned is forearmed!*

Savvy Strategy 36: Overcome Personal Depression and Despair

It is a fact that nearly everyone in the helping professions is subject to bouts of self-defeating thoughts. Depression might be too strong a word, but after a long day of seeing troubled young people, life can look less than rosy. After weeks of such days, and a particularly sad episode with a student who rejects assistance, it is hard to keep "the black dog" at bay. Consequently, if you have chosen to work in such an environment, you need emotional survival skills, and here are a few:

1. Try "chair yoga." It provides relaxation for muscles stiffened by sitting at a desk too long.
2. Try a "positive hour." That's sixty minutes during which you think only positive thoughts, say only positive things, and hear only positive things. Sounds simple. Hard to do! Takes practice—and discipline.
3. Involve others in your positive hour. Maybe recruit students who can list all the positive things they have discovered through counseling. Maybe involve a circle of friends who want to have fun with a new mental discipline.
4. Make a list of problems that plague you. Opposite each, make a plan for resolving them. Maybe the plans are humorous. That's even better, because laughing at yourself is healthy!
5. Maintain and review a tally of all the positive accomplishments over the past months or weeks. That can break inertia and get you going.

6. Give yourself a treat—a special movie, a museum, a favorite dinner, or an undisturbed nap.
7. Avoid news programs for a day (but otherwise stay informed).
8. Consider organizing some new routines and a more comfortable structure.
9. Exercise in a gym or, preferably, outside. Get friends to join you.
10. Volunteer for some nontraditional activities that can give you a new perspective on your situation and concerns.
11. Develop a "to-do" list that prioritizes issues with which you need to deal—and provide a set of dates when you will work on each.

People in high-stress jobs (and that might mean most people these days) and those with medical problems will be affected by the weight of their concern for negative elements in their lives. One physician at the Sloan-Kettering Cancer Center and another at the Center for Mind-Body Medicine (both in New York) assert that depression is natural—but so is working it out. You have to take responsibility for your own mental health—which, in the counseling field, is one of your most potent tools.

When you review the list above, you will find that each has something in common. They reflect the truth in the imperative, "Just do it!" That logo of a sports equipment manufacturer is rooted in the restorative power of honoring the mind-body connection—and taking positive actions. Pay attention!

Motto: *When it rains, remember where you left the umbrella!*

Savvy Strategy 37: Work with Parents!

Interviews with more than one hundred counselors confirm that working with parents and helping them work with their children is always among the top five priority concerns. Dealing with parents is often thought to be more difficult and introduces new and troublesome variables into the counseling process. But remember this:

1. Parents want their children to succeed.
2. They worry when their children "need counseling."
3. They usually have problems other than the child you are seeing.
4. The child is unlikely to be able to change without parental support.
5. Parents can help or hinder achievement of your goals for the child.
6. Most parents are interested in hearing about their children.
7. Most parents appreciate guidance from a professional.

8. Many parents work several jobs and can use all the help they can get.
9. Everyone in urban America is busy.
10. Counselors and parents should be on the same side, collaborating!

When meeting parents, give them the facts. "I invited you to meet because . . ." Tell them that their help is needed in solving the problem their child is confronting, and share with them any documentation (grades, teacher/school nurse evaluations, etc.) that frames the child's area(s) of difficulty. Then, listen to their concerns and reactions to the information they have received.

Help them separate issues and offer suggestions for shaping the behavior(s) being discussed. Ask for their support to ensure the success of their child. Where statistics are available and relate to the child's problem, provide something in writing the parents can read at home. (Example: One child in five is sexually active before age fifteen.) Or, if fatigue seems to be the problem, let the parents know that at least nine hours of sleep each night is recommended by medical and child-development experts. If you feel self-conscious about telling parents about child rearing, remember that most have spent more time in driver education classes than in classes to learn how to be an effective parent!

Some children are overscheduled, with too many activities that distract them from their studies. Also, parental emphasis on extracurricular activities (soccer moms and football fathers) can unintentionally devalue academic effort. As always, parents will be hypersensitive to anything that sounds like criticism of them, so phrase your comments carefully in order to inform and not to indict. Be prepared for resistance and resentment. They may be more uneasy than you are!

Motto: *Counselor, become a friend of the family!*

Savvy Strategy 38: Promote Financial Fitness

Financial literacy is overlooked in most school curricula. It's hard to develop business people when most have no knowledge of how money works, how companies make money, and how single parents can survive when needs outstrip means. Looking realistically at the future, this is especially important for female students (although probably it would be politically incorrect to say that).

Possibly in collaboration with a math or business teacher, counselors could introduce the game Product in a Box, from which students imagine, create a product, and establish a business to sell the product. Some business basics are presented, along with insights into the work ethic of the students, their values, and their understanding of work and money. You may find, as others have, that girls lag behind boys in developing interest in finances.

To close that gap, two books are recommended as the basis for discussion in study groups for girls. *No More Frogs to Kiss: 99 Ways to Give Economic Power to Girls* by Joline Godfrey is one; *Our Wildest Dreams: Women Entrepreneurs Making Money, Having Fun, Doing Good*, also by Joline Godfrey, is the other.

Counselors might want to be alert to articles in local papers and popular business magazines that emphasize the achievements of young entrepreneurs. Perhaps a careers bulletin board could be developed for such materials, as well as job opportunities from local employers. Once a program has been established to promote business understanding, there may be an opportunity for internships for some students.

One of the most valuable business books available is Jack Stack's easy-to-read *The Great Game of Business*. He describes how he answered this important question: How can you expect people to help you make money for your company when people don't know how companies make money? Stack's company, Springfield ReManufacturing, rebuilds automotive and truck engines—dirty, hard, noisy work that involves mostly people with only a high school education or less. They have been incredibly successful. Thousands of visitors from other companies have come to see how a miracle in manufacturing and business skills was created. Along with all the academically based programs, maybe it would be okay to include some business education for your clients.

Motto: *Be bullish on finances!*

Savvy Strategy 39: Nourish Thinking Skills

Thinking is a skill quite separate from intelligence. This old story makes that point. A professor has a flat tire next to a mental hospital. He spills all the lug nuts into a sewer. He is in despair, but an inmate speaks through a barred window, "Just take one lug nut from each of the other three wheels, and you can drive away." The professor is surprised by the wonderful suggestion, but the inmate replies, "I'm in here because I'm crazy, not stupid."

This is an important point in a culture that emphasizes speed in completing tasks ("Hurry and finish your homework so we can watch TV") instead of thinking through processes to solutions. As a result, many leave school with nearly zero analytic skills. Some concepts to master (often called thinking skills and addressed by many authors):

1. *Analyzing* to separate events from processes;
2. *Discriminating* to differentiate among values and assumptions;
3. *Summarizing* to collect facts into simple statements;
4. *Focusing* on key points rather than the surrounding chatter;
5. *Observing* actions and reactions for relationships;
6. *Classifying* items and events to see groupings or *profiling*;
7. *Interpreting* data to infer meaning based on experience; and
8. *Deciding* on the basis of evidence and experience.

To have fun with these ideas, consider the books of Edward de Bono, the British guru of creativity and thinking skills. He is employed at astronomical fees by corporations to consult on technical problems and to teach scientists and engineers how to "break through" their training to become creative and innovative. Yet his books are easy to read and widely available in paperback editions.

There is a story about an Eastern European railroad. During Soviet times, all decisions were made in Moscow, relayed to an intermediate field office, and then to the railroad. More than a dozen years after the Soviet occupation ended, none of the fourteen thousand railroad employees knew how to make business decisions. An extreme example, perhaps, but when people are not encouraged to develop thinking/analytic skills, those abilities atrophy—even among university graduates.

Make your counselees think! Involve them in analysis of their situations, ask them to find the patterns that produce problems, and insist that they interpret and "own" the cause and effect relationships that have put them in your office. They will benefit more from the experience, and they will have begun to develop new skills for a lifetime of effective problem solving and decision making.

Motto: *Think about it—and discover the marvels of analysis!*

Savvy Strategy 40: Understand the Power of Culture

Several years ago, there was said to be a high school in Los Angeles in which students spoke thirty-nine different "native" languages. For each language, there is a host culture, with mores and folkways that are dramatically different from those of other cultures. What is culture, anyway? It is the sea of habits, practices, foods, gestures, and history that we swim in. Our cultures shape us, tell us what is okay, what behaviors are rewarded, and which are forbidden. How can we make schools in general and the counseling office culture free?

In fact, you cannot, because there is a predominant American or Anglo culture in most schools, while in others many aspects of Hispanic or African American cultures may be seen. But despite that, school district rules and learning goals must be the primary shaper and enforcer of school cultures in which all students have to perform and conform if they are to be successful. Generally speaking, it is the classroom teachers who must be the primary buffers against "culture shock," but it is up to the counselor to intervene when cultural clashes create difficulties for individuals and entire classes. That can be difficult work.

However, as with all situations, counselors do not have unlimited options in spelling out behavioral choices and consequences, and neither do students in deciding to go along and get along. Sometimes the most difficult situation for counselors is providing protection for students who are being abused because of their cultural requirements. (Note the recent furor in France and Germany about headscarves and other religious symbols in schools.)

Meanwhile, the primary skill counselors must rely on is listening—and asking the questions that lead to understanding the causative issue for the student(s). Then it is a matter of explaining school district rules and the limits within which compliance will be assessed. Often, foreign nationals can cope better with rude behavior from locals if they can be helped to see the differences culture makes. And sometimes, rude locals can become more accepting when traditional differences are explained. Otherwise, locals are not exempt from requirements for acceptable behavior.

Counselors must model truly democratic behavior in accepting all students and assisting students in seeing past the differences among their peers. Celebrating differences is useful, but the school's learning goals must be priority one.

Motto: *Knowing about the person helps to know the person.*

Savvy Strategy 41: Master Listening!

Several decades back, there were two distinct philosophies of counseling. One was *directive*, based on the fact that schools operated in loco parentis and that students had to know the rules, conform to them, or leave the school. The polar opposite was *nondirective*, in which listening was more important than telling and that students would come to understand and accept the rules if they are allowed to think through them. The thinking goes something like this: the client always knows the right answer and will come up with it if allowed to do so. So said Carl Rogers.

Well, the pressures of time seem to force many counselors into the telling, directive role. Some opt for it because they like it, some because they do not know how to listen and are uncomfortable with the silences real listening involves.

Choice: Do you want to be known as the counselor with all the answers, or the counselor who actually listens and engages *with* the counselee? As always, options available to students are not unlimited, so why waste time letting them fumble through to a decision? The reason, of course, is that the student gains additional insights when given the time (a couple of extra minutes) to muddle through to an answer that fits. That s/he chose. That s/he owns and acts upon.

Sometimes, we "know" the student's problem. What we do not know is: *why can't the student see it?* And the only way to get that answer is to listen. When we take time to allow the student to explain how s/he got to such a different answer, occasionally there is an opportunity to correct a misunderstanding that frees the student to other problem-solving breakthroughs—and to build your reputation as a counselor who cares enough to listen.

People who listen, who know how to separate the words from the music, to hear what is being omitted as well as what is being said, have access to an enormous amount of information. They can respond with insight to the speaker, who often is so stunned that s/he has been heard that the rest of the story comes tumbling out.

This works everywhere, not just with students and teachers. Master managers and administrators know how to listen, know when they're hearing the truth, know when they're in the presence of confident people or people who are faking. And that's what kids see so often—that the adults around them are faking it, not listening, not caring, quick to provide pat answers and canned solutions.

Motto: *When you care about someone, you really listen!*

Savvy Strategy 42: Understand Discipline!

Counseling often only comes down to discipline. Teachers think they lack it, students can't hack it, principals wonder if they can back it, parents want to whack it, and counselors want to sack it. But there it is, like an elephant in the living room. You cannot ignore it. And until you understand it, discipline will haunt you!

As many young counselors discover, their office becomes the dumping ground for teachers' discipline problems. Later, though, it will turn out that the teacher is the one with the problem; that student misbehavior was a result of teacher confusion about discipline, about his/her personal style, and a resulting inconsistency.

A generation ago, Charles H. Wolfgang and Carl D. Glickman provided a model and questionnaire for discipline management with three faces. First was the *interventionist*, the teacher who makes all the rules; second was the *interactionist*, who shared rule making with students; and third was the *noninterventionist*, who abdicated rule making and let the students decide. Each style has its advocates: interventionists—James Dobson and Teresa Hessman; interactionists—William Glasser and Richard Dreikurs; and noninterventionists—Tom Gordon and Carl Rogers. Help teachers discover their preferred style—and understand if it has to be adjusted.

With current school discipline issues, including widespread cheating, vandalism, sexual promiscuity and abuse, foul language, bigotry, violence, and substance abuse, some systemwide decisions need to be made. Otherwise it will be impossible to increase test scores and academic achievement and provide the foundation for leadership in the generation ahead. Systemwide decisions need to be made by all constituents of the system, and that would include parents, nonparent taxpayers, employers, judiciary, media, students, teachers, and administrators. Without that support base, current problems can only get worse.

In the meantime, perhaps the most important things counselors can do is to empower teachers to take control of their classrooms; to work with teachers to develop control styles that are congruent with their interpersonal styles; and to help them involve student leaders in developing their skills by marshalling student support around goals that matter to young people and are consistent with school district objectives. See Ron Clark's book, *The Essential 55*, that reports on using rules and courtesy techniques to turn his North Carolina classroom around. Good stuff!

Motto: *Grace under pressure is the mark of a civilized person.*

Savvy Strategy 43: Recognize Generational Values

One of the best training videos ever made is *What You Are Is Where You Were When*. A maverick professor of economics turned college administrator turned comedic management educator named Morris Massey galvanized audiences with his grasp of values programming across generations. Like other theorists, he said that you become you pretty early in life. To understand your value orientation, you need to consider the adults around you during your formative years.

It was a broad sketch of styles and preferences, but live and video audiences easily found themselves in his presentations. And laughed. And understood cross-generational dynamics better. Short synopsis: Do not explain student behavior to parents in terms of the student's values. You have to hook into the parents' values to be understood. Better yet, you need to mirror the parents' values (regardless of your age) to be heard without intergenerational static.

Two other sources to check out are *Generations: The History of America's Future, 1584 to 2069* by Neil Howe and William Strauss, and "Generations Theory: Counseling Using Generational Value Systems" by Colette Dollarhide and Robyn Haxton, in the *Journal of the California Association of Counseling and Development*. The authors offered this analysis of values:

- GI generation, born 1901–1924; Values: teamwork, collective energy, authority, optimism.
- Silent generation, born 1925–1942; Values: expertise, process, dialogue, equality, participation, personal communications, feelings.
- Boomer generation, born 1943–1960; Values: self-awareness, critical thinking, individual achievement, variety, mobility.
- 13th generation (Gen X), born 1951–1981; Values: honesty, pragmatism, independence, self-reliance.
- Millennial generation, born 1982–2004 (approx.); Values: expected to be the same as the GI generation.

So what does all this mean? We know that education is generally designed for the past generation. That means Gen X values are being applied to the millennial generation. The question arises with the times, calling for higher structure—are we ready to provide it? Knowing that conflict could readily exist, prepare. Knowing where differences might occur will be a big help.

Motto: *Helping the generations learn from each other and communicate is an important role.*

Savvy Strategy 44: Promote Joy and Happiness

Popular pop psychologist Dennis Prager wrote that *Happiness Is a Serious Problem*. More recently, Martin Seligman wrote about *Authentic Happiness*. So, what is it about happiness that is so mysterious, so elusive?

It may be that descriptions of happiness promoted by TV and its glamorous ads represent artificial and unattainable goals. It may be that in the current environment of technological change that is essentially redefining all jobs and professions, happiness is becoming more elusive. We see downsizing and fewer "good" jobs, corporate graft, increased cost of housing and utilities, increased pressure for grades, and the appearance of a new class system based on technological acumen. Really, few among previous generations know how to be helpful as they are the primary victims of wholesale changes. PhDs working at Wal-Mart?

Counselors can provide a counterpoint to all of the clamor. It may be that counselors and a few authors are the only professionals promoting mental health as defined by self-esteem, curiosity, bravery, spirituality, humor, kindness, leadership, and humility. Increasingly, many are seeing the positive correlation between helping others and feeling better about oneself.

Maybe with all the social, economic, and political turmoil in society, happiness will most readily be achieved by doing for and with others, rediscovering collaboration and contribution, and focusing on self-satisfaction rather than the acquisition of material goods.

Again, counselors are called upon to be role models. When students meet a counselor who is enjoying the role, who is upbeat and positive, who helps cast personal problems into a solvable perspective, and who laughs easily, there is a counterpoint, an alternative to the doom and gloom of the mass media.

The lessons counselors can provide really have two points of perspective: priorities and price. That is, confronting students with the questions: (1) What are your priorities right now? and (2) What is that costing you? That comes down to choices and balancing small sacrifices in the present with rewards and a broader range of choices/options in the future.

No matter how logical that is, there must be some measure of joy and happiness in the present to make the sacrifices for the future possible and tolerable. Show kids how to be happy today while preparing for the future. Deferred gratification doesn't sell. Pleasure now does. Perspective!

Motto: *Don't allow youth to be wasted on the young!*

Savvy Strategy 45: Confront Child Abuse!

To refresh your memory, you are a *mandated reporter of child abuse*. You have no option but to report by phone to the police or child services department (as directed by your school district), and to file a written report within thirty-six hours. This is a responsibility you share with other educational professionals. But, because of your training in observing and listening to children, you may be the first to pick up on the emotional pain or physical discomfort abuse can cause.

Abuse of children is not just physical or sexual. Neglect and emotional abuse can be equally damaging. Slapping a child's hand for deliberately damaging another's painting may be poor disciplinary practice, but it is not child abuse. But the use of push-ups or other physical exercise to the point of pain as a punishment is abusive. So what, exactly is abuse? What are its signs? What should teachers, counselors, and others be aware of, and alert to? This is one of the times when connecting with community resources can be especially important. Get a local expert to brief your school staff on this important issue.

There are many books on the subject, but one that is really helpful is *Child Abuse: Educators' Responsibilities*. This book eliminates any ambiguity about what you must do. Not only educators, but parents, too, need to know.

Since report cards often are the trigger that unleashes parental abuse of a child, the Child Abuse Council Coordination Project provides special fliers that can be distributed to parents with report cards. The advice it provides is heartbreaking in its simplicity: Sit down with the child to review the report card. Find something to praise. Stay calm. Ask the child how you can help improve the grades. Ask what the child can do. Make a plan. Follow up and support the child.

When a child shows up in your office (or elsewhere in the school) wearing the signs of abuse, you must ask gentle but direct questions. "Where did you get that bruise, Tommy? Did someone hit you? It must have hurt a lot. Would you tell me who did that to you?"

While counselors are NOT required to investigate, if you can elicit confirming information before you call the police, so much the better. In any event, the child needs to know that such injuries, neglect, or emotional abuse cannot go unreported; that no one has the right to inflict that kind of pain; and that the authorities will protect the child. Dark moments for any counselor.

Motto: *It shouldn't hurt to be a kid!*

Savvy Strategy 46: Incorporate Ethics into Your Professional Activities

Now let us take time to consider ethics, that most difficult of subjects. Rotary International, a service club for business men and women, made the subject a little easier by formulating "The Four-Way Test of What We Say and Do." Four short questions follow: (1) Is it the TRUTH? (2) Is it FAIR to all concerned? (3) Is it BENEFICIAL to all concerned? (4) Will it build GOODWILL and better friendships? So many ethical breaches, minor and major, might be avoided if the people involved stop to ask themselves these questions.

At its base, ethical behavior means not putting others at an unfair disadvantage. It means older kids should not take advantage of younger children. It means studying hard to score well on an exam is okay, but paying for a copy of the test is unethical. It means not taking more than your share, nor lying to gain advantage. It means, finally, treating everyone fairly and with respect. Simple.

Counselors are provided codes of ethics and ethical guidance by national (American Counseling Association [ACA]) and state-level (California Association of Counseling and Development [CACD]) professional organizations. Among the items common to most are:

- Don't claim professional qualifications you don't have;
- Recognize the boundaries of your competence;
- Don't misuse the power of your position; and
- Keep your personal issues out of the counseling relationship.

When you check these four items against the four Rotary tests, the relationships are compelling. Maybe all ethical issues reduce to the Golden Rule—treating others the way we want to be treated. Why does something so obvious have to be so difficult? Because we live with a lot of pressure to acquire and to achieve, and the ends often are more important than the means.

Motto: *Let's stand together on firm ground to build a great tomorrow!*

Savvy Strategy 47: Support Beginning Teachers

Throughout this book there have been references to supporting teachers. This Strategy, however, puts its emphasis on working with beginning teachers, whether they're fresh out of college or someone with gray hair entering a second career. These people need help so that they do not suffer burnout, as have so many of those who were just a few years ahead.

Young teachers don't leave because they don't understand the curriculum, can't write a lesson plan, can't follow a textbook's teacher's guide, or suddenly decide they don't like working with young people. They leave because they are disenchanted.

They leave because they feel overwhelmed by paperwork, daunted by discipline, fearful of observations, left out by colleagues, stressed out by lack of supplies and materials, intimidated by parents, threatened by time requirements, and ignorant of school district policies and procedures. With this load of negative impressions and feelings, it's no wonder that people leave the profession!

Since counselors have the freedom to talk to anyone in the school, why not focus on the young teachers? Why not invite them for coffee in your office after school? Why not open a conversation about their problems and frustrations? Why not identify the issues that are common to all of them—information that no one else will have—and organize a response. Perhaps the key person is the school secretary, or maybe it's the principal. But what a grand favor you do for everyone when you take the initiative to anticipate problems and solve them! The entire school— from students to custodians—benefits!

As is so often the case when people are frustrated, the causes are so obvious that they are hard to see. For example, what so many new teachers want to know is:

- What's required in terms of observations, records, and lesson plans;
- What's the grading policy;
- Tips for working with an irate parent; and
- Discipline tips for handling a difficult class.

Often these subjects are not covered by academic courses. In fact, they cannot be, because the issues are rooted in the situation, in the school. And who can better deal with them than the school counselor? Reach out and save a career!

Motto: *Experience is a great teacher, but it can be received vicariously!*

Savvy Strategy 48: Speak Well and Convincingly

Think of all the songs you love to sing and remember. What makes them so special? The words and the music fit together! In a word, there is *congruence* that communicates to you—and to millions of others. When we speak—to peers, students, anyone—they listen for that congruence. We say we like, respect, and want to help others, but what do they *feel* when they hear and see us speak to them? Is there a single message of caring and concern? Or are there several messages? Like "Thank God this is the last student of the day" and "I'm here to help you if I can, but this doesn't look hopeful." Words and music communicate.

Unfortunately, some counselors deal with this issue by lapsing into professional jargon, using a vocabulary that is clearly out of place in a dialogue between an adult professional and a student, or, equally inappropriate, is the counselor's decision to use the argot of the streets, the current "in" words, or referring to counselees in overly familiar terms (like "Bro" or "Man" or "Girl").

It is the professional's responsibility to *communicate*—using words and terms that the counselee can understand but also are acceptable in "polite society"; that is, language that is not offensive or "dumbed down." If you speak clearly, slowly, and check for understanding as often as needed, it is unlikely you will ever talk about things the counselee cannot understand. There is no need to use "obdurate" instead of stubborn or "chronic mental indolent" instead of intellectually lazy or indifferent. Not with teachers or administrators, either!

Sometimes individuals have disturbing speech mannerisms that distract the listener—too many ums, aahs, you knows, like, you understand what I'm saying. How to change? Record your voice. Listen to the recording. Ask others to listen. Practice. Professionals do this, the people who make "voice-overs" for TV ads and are the voices for radio ads.

Speaking always is a performance, and all performances should be audience sensitive. Pay attention! Are people listening, or looking away? Are they with you, or somewhere else? Do they care about what you're saying? Do they care about you? Your effectiveness as a counselor depends on affirmative answers to these questions.

And a final point: Keep your statements short, which is made easier if you don't repeat yourself, saying the same thing three ways, three times. Clean, clear, crisp—and congruent! Anyone who cares can do it!

Motto: *"Well said!" is a compliment indeed!*

Savvy Strategy 49: Maintain High Expectations

Recently, the *Wall Street Journal* reported that ". . . no less than 497 studies have shown that teachers' expectations affect how students do. . . ." Then there are the famous studies by UCLA professor Robert Rosenthal and Lenore Jacobson (*Pigmalion in the Classroom*, 175–76) who told teachers that a group of students had scored exceptionally high on a test, which predicted intellectual blooming and would likely indicate that the students would perform well in class. In fact, the students were chosen at random and high-performance fabricated. But, because the teachers expected high performance, the students demonstrated statistically significant gains over other classmates. A classic case of performance rising to meet expectations.

The power of positive expectations has been with us in all of recorded history, but most people never are exposed to it; or, if they know about it, they have experienced it in such short-term ways that its power is never realized. All serious athletes know about this. Some medical clinics combine mental imagery with modern medicine to effect "miraculous" cures. And a friend with multiple sclerosis, who has kept her disease in remission for almost forty years, will leave the room if someone speaks negatively about anyone or anything. Even sleep counselors recommend avoiding the late news before going to bed. Negative energy limits, inhibits!

For some, being positive seems "natural," because they always are. But it is a choice people make. This is an appeal, counselor, for you to make that choice, to be a source of positive energy for others in the school.

But maybe most of all, counselors need to be fountains of positive expectancy for the students with whom they work. Even when students want to achieve goals that seem impossible, counselors have an obligation not to diminish those dreams but to feed them with enthusiasm and information and, always, the expectancy of success! Success, as a poster says, is a frame of mind, a way of thinking, the replacement of every doubt with a "can do" spirit that makes failure unlikely!

But more than positive expectations, counselors need to ensure that their clients get *success-producing tools*—understanding goals, objectives, targets, and the power of planning as a success-assurance tool. Also important is follow-up, maintaining the nurturing, supportive, positive feedback that fuels achievers.

However, that is where success systems tend to break down—follow-up and follow-through from people who are too busy to remember to reward, to praise, to encourage. Getting teachers, parents, and others in the student's sphere to provide these success reinforcers should be a priority task for counselors.

Motto: *Believe goals can be achieved.*

Savvy Strategy 50: Know How to Say Goodbye

Counselors, like others, relocate for personal and professional reasons. It is a matter of professional courtesy and discipline to make it easy for your replacement to pick up the work you have in process, both with students and programs. Few things are more damaging to a program than a change in leadership that is chaotic, which is to say, unplanned.

Therefore, when a change in counselors is planned, there are some things to do to protect the investment in program development and to ensure the integrity of the information acquired in working with students, faculty, and parents.

First, ensure that your files are organized. Type a note that explains to your replacement the filing system you used and from which administrator the key(s) can be obtained. Make sure there is no breach in security or confidentiality.

Second, type notes for distribution to faculty, students, and parents with whom you have worked. Time these for release the day before you leave. Make sure your farewell note praises the school and celebrates achievements of the program. Also, if you can, use those notes to introduce your replacement and, of course, ask that the same levels of courtesy and support that you have received be accorded to that person. These notes can be humorous, but they must be upbeat and make people feel good (although they may be sad to see you go).

Third, close out all ongoing client services and ensure case files contain all relevant data so your replacement can continue with clients if they wish. Where possible, bring cases to closure, but do not rush students who need more time.

Fourth, schedule meetings on the last day with students and faculty (separately) with whom you have worked especially closely, and shortly before you leave, meet with your principal or administrator to turn over keys and any necessary documents. Then take your leave without further fanfare or celebration—unless your boss has planned one for you.

And for the students you leave behind? Another life lesson. There are beginnings and endings. Sometimes people leave for a short while, sometimes forever. On that note, be careful about leaving a forwarding address or personal contact data. You may find that you have a persistent admirer, and that can become a problem. So step through the door into a new future—without baggage.

Motto: *A time to come, a time to go!*

The Great Counselor Questionnaire

1. Do you have adequate professional training?
2. Do you know who you are professionally?
3. Do you love what you're doing?
4. Do others seem to like what you're doing?
5. Do you enjoy listening more than talking?
6. Do you have a written plan (that you wrote) for what you do?
7. Do you have specific goals for the day/year and for each counselee?
8. Do you speak clearly?
9. Do you have an advisory team(s)?
10. Do you have a specialty (e.g., a course you teach; area in which you excel)?
11. Do you know about funding and budgets?
12. Do you know how to destress yourself?
13. Do you keep up your skills?
14. Do you know how to evaluate your work (are most of your goals achieved)?
15. Do you know how to get what you want (office space, books, supplies)?
16. Do you know how to publicize your skills?
17. Do you belong to professional organizations?
18. Do you know how to get along with others?
19. Do you have a mentor?
20. Do you know when and how to say goodbye?

Answering yes to all twenty means you're well on your way toward being a very great counselor!

Selected Bibliography for Counselors

American Psychological Association Monitor 29, 12 (December 1998): 30.

Bauman, Sheri. *Cyberbullying: What Counselors Need to Know*. American Counseling Association, 2010 (Contact information: 800-422-2648, ext. 222).

Borba, Michele. *Character Builders (A Series for K–6)*. Carson, CA: Jalmar Press, 1998.

Brown, Erika. "When Rich Kids Go Bad." *Forbes* (October 14, 2002): 140–48.

Canfield, Jack, and H. Wells. *100 Ways to Enhance Self-Concept in the Classroom*. New York: Prentice Hall, 1976.

Carnegie, Dale. *How to Win Friends and Influence People*. New York: Pocket Books, 1936, 1981 (and later editions).

Clements, Andrew. *Jake Drake: Bully Buster*. New York: Aladdin/Simon & Schuster, 2000.

Curry, J. F. "Specific Psychotherapies for Childhood and Adolescent Depression." *Biological Psychiatry* 49, 12 (June 15, 2001): 1091–1100.

de Bono, Edward. *Masterthinker: Your Easy Guide to Innovative Thinking*. Larchmont, NY: International Center for Creative Thinking, Inc., 1985 (One of many books by Dr. de Bono, who holds an MD and multiple PhD degrees.).

Glickman, Carl D., and Charles H. Wolfgang. *Solving Discipline Problems*. Boston: Allyn & Bacon, 1987.

Hegarty, Christopher (with Philip Goldberg). *How to Manage Your Boss*. New York: Rawson Wade, 1980.

Independent Means Products. (Contact: 1-800-350-1816).

International Journal for Biosocial Research 2, 1–9 (1981) (Article on impact of wall color on difficult children, including mixing instructions, by Alexander G. Schauss, American Institute for Biosocial Research, Tacoma, WA.).

Lang, Robert M. "The Hidden Dress Code Dilemma." *Clearinghouse* 59, 6 (February 1986): 277–79.
Mohandie, Kris. *School Violence Threat Management: A Practical Guide for Educators, Law Enforcement, and Mental Health Professionals.* San Diego: Specialized Training Services, 2000.
Mohandie, Kris, and C. Hatcher. "Suicide and Violence Risk in Law Enforcement: Practical Guidelines for Risk Assessment, Prevention, and Intervention." *Behavioral Science and the Law* 17: 357–76, 1999.
National Campaign to Prevent Teen Pregnancy Report, Washington, DC (May 19, 2003).
New York Times (March 24, 2002): 24, cols. 1–4.
New York Times (September 4, 2001): D8, col. 4 (re: National Heart, Lung, and Blood Institute report that children require nine hours of sleep daily).
Podemski, Richard S., and John H. Chandler Jr. "Psychological Contracting for the Counselor's Role: Procedures for Counselors and Principals." *The School Counselor* (January 1982): 183–88.
Slaikeu, Karl A. *Crisis Intervention: A Handbook for Practice and Research.* University of Texas at Austin: Allyn & Bacon, Inc., 1985.
Stack, Jack (with Bo Burlingham). *The Great Game of Business.* New York: Currency/Doubleday, 1992.
Suicide Prevention in California Public Schools. California State Department of Education, Sacramento, 1980.
U.S. *Journal RIE.* Research Report 143 (November 1992).

While not referenced specifically in this volume, each of the authors has produced books valuable to counselors and other school personnel.
Blanchard, Kenneth, and Normal Vincent Peale. *The Power of Ethical Management.* New York: Fawcett Crest, 1991.
Child Abuse Council's Coordination Project, Sacramento, CA (1990).
Child Abuse: Educators' Responsibilities. Crime Prevention Center, Office of the Attorney General, Sacramento, CA (1990).
Clark, Ron. *The Essential 55.* New York: Hyperion Press, 2004.
Dollarhide, Collette, and Robyn Haxton. "Generations Theory: Counseling Using Generational Value Systems." *California Association for Counseling and Development* 19 (1998–99): 21–27.
Fulfilling Prophecy: Further Evidence for Pygmalion and their Mediating Mechanisms. New York: MSS Modular, 1974.
Massey, Morris. *What You Are Is Where You Were When.* Video Enterprise Media: Cambridge, MA, 1975.
Prager, Dennis. *Happiness Is a Serious Problem.* New York: Harper Collins, 1998.
Rosenthal, Robert, and Lenore Jacobson. *Pygmalion in the Classroom: Teacher Expectations and Pupil Intellectual Development.* New York: Holt, Rinehart & Winston, 1968.
Seligman, Martin. *Authentic Happiness.* New York: Free Press, 2002.
Strauss, W., and N. Howe. *Generations: The History of America's Future.* New York: William Morrow Co., 1991.

To the Principal

For most any program or person to be successful in reaching their goals they need a little—or perhaps more than a little—help from above. This fact can be seen very clearly in many aspects of life—the nurturing parent, the successful child, the caring doctor, the healthy patient, the fine tutor/teacher, the achieving student. Would Franklin Roosevelt be the successful adult without his mother, Sara Delano Roosevelt; Helen Keller without her teacher, Annie Sullivan; UCLA teams without John Wooden; the Green Bay Packers without Vince Lombardi; and the New York Yankees without Joe Torre?

When the team doesn't do well, often it's the coach or leader who's fired; on the psychiatrist's couch it's often the parent who's blamed; and in the hospital, when the patient worsens (check the medical insurance rates), the doctor is blamed. It's not easy being the leader, but it does bring rewards and gives one a fabulous feeling of power and achievement, responsibility, and control—especially, of course, when things improve and when goals are reached.

The school principal is the major, identified leader in school. Holding ultimate responsibility for the success of all programs, yet unlike the business CEO to which she is often compared, she does not hold control over all the variables that make up the business. The story is told of teachers and principals in a district attending a motivational meeting, in which a successful entrepreneur told how, by diligence, stick-to-itiveness, and hard work, he turned a rundown bakery business into a million-dollar blueberry muffin business. Finally, a rather experienced teacher raised her hand and asked, "What do you do when you're delivered a bruised and broken crate of blueberries?," and the entrepreneur stated, "We send them back. We want only the best for our customers, and that's what's made us so successful." "Well," said the teacher, "we don't do that. We accept all the 'blueberries' we are sent, even the broken and bruised, and we try to make them into the very best so that they, too, can have a chance to be successful."

Today's principals need to use every asset—teachers, counselors, and coaches—given to them to help see them through to victory. Oftentimes, victory is defined for them as being the domain of instruction alone, but in an open letter to the mayor of Los Angeles from the UCLA Center for Mental Health in the Schools, the writers state, "Good instruction, of course, is essential . . . But, better instruction alone cannot ensure that all students have an equal opportunity to succeed at school." The letter goes on to plead for a focus on the development of a policy that would bring together all resources that would address the barriers to learning—resources including not only instructional services but also all support services. Counselors would clearly be part of this picture. Bringing the counselors more closely into the school instructional effort and team should be a major goal for all school principals.

It is the goal of the principal's section of the book to provide you, the school principal, with some successful techniques, procedures, and strategies for doing just that. Of course, it's not expected that you use all of the strategies (one can, of course, hope!), but it is useful to try to include some of these suggestions each year, perhaps with the sincere hope that these strategies will help make your "blueberry muffins" the best in the world!

THE PRINCIPAL'S ROLE

The Principal's Role

Savvy Strategy 51: Participate Early in the Hiring Process

Try to pick the best blueberries from the start. Many principals will "inherit" staff, and we'll address that later. But now, let's imagine you can have a hand in the selection of a new counselor(s). First step—talk to yourself. Ask what you want in a school counselor. What do you want them to do? What do you want them to accomplish?

Do you have preferences regarding behavior, dress, or language (bilingual)? Do you feel they should be mainly involved in supporting the instructional program, providing sessions regarding study habits, or test preparation? Do you feel they should serve as a major supporter to the teachers in terms of discipline, control, and improving attendance? Or should they be a major supporter of parents—providing workshops for parents on strategies for "perfect parenting," "selecting a college," "being a stepparent"? Do you feel the counselor should be mainly a *student* advocate—providing group sessions for students on age-appropriate issues, being available for students facing a crisis, or just being there for students who wish to talk to an adult who has expertise in helping them make decisions? Or do you want all of the above?

In the best possible world, perhaps—but not likely. In our world as it exists today it would almost be impossible for one person to have a major impact on all of those areas. Counselors at the elementary and junior high school especially often try to do all those things and spread themselves too thin, with little success to show for their efforts. After you have pulled together a picture of the type of counselor you want and the areas (prioritize) in which you want them to focus, *write it down*. It is important to have a clear picture in your mind and on paper regarding the person you want to hire to do the job in your school.

When you are clear about that and exactly what you want, then get involved with the district hiring officer or personnel department. Share your wishes with them. Express an interest in approving the person to be selected. Be involved in the notice announcing the availability of the position, and help develop what qualifications are to be mentioned, what training and certification is called for, what experience is required, and what references are requested.

Most personnel departments will be delighted with your involvement and understanding of the importance of their work. After all, they're examining the first cut of the blueberries! By coming into them with some written statements regarding what you need, you're helping them meet those needs and are not making them guess at what may best be to your advantage. Even if the "search" for new staff must be limited to within the district, your doing some of the preliminary work will show your commitment to the selection and your concern that the best possible person be obtained for the position.

In addition, your involvement will signal your concern to the personnel department and others (you know how word travels) about how important this position is in your estimation and how important you consider it to the achievement of your school's goals. What a morale booster to counselors throughout the district!

Motto: *Well begun is half done.*

Savvy Strategy 52: Use the Interview as a Launching Pad

Interviewing candidates for the counseling position at your school is an important opportunity to establish a successful program at your school. Not only are you interviewing but also you're selling yourself as a leader, supervisor, innovator, and an educational advocate. You're looking to employ this person, but you're also looking to determine if you can work well with this person (if there is an indefinable bond)—someone you can depend on, learn from, and achieve success with—for your school programs.

You shouldn't have to learn to like this person. There are many other things you two will have to achieve; that shouldn't be one of them. You should feel a liking for this person right at the start. This should be a person from whom you can learn.

They should know more about counseling than you, and this should not be someone who feels they "fly by the seat of their pants" when working with students. They should be aware of specific theories, programs, processes, and successful techniques and procedures already available to meet the specific counseling goals of your school. In other words, they should have a body of knowledge available to them in their specific area.

You might want to take some time to check the references of the person you're about to select—not only the written ones—but a follow-up call to that person, or someone you know personally who was at the candidate's previous work site or training site. You should also share with the candidate that you might do this if they have no objections. Of course, this should be cleared with the personnel department, also.

This might come across as picky and unfair and too much extra work. *But* (and of course there is a but) too many principals work and work and work some more to try to remove an unsatisfactory staff member. Perhaps a little more effort at the beginning would be much more worthwhile and less painful to all parties concerned. Of course, there are some things that cannot be gleaned from curriculum vitae and reference checks, and it is my feeling that in the counseling profession special intangibles cannot be put aside.

As an administrator one would want to be able to feel that the school counselor was operating from a strong intellectual base in his or her profession, but also from a strong personal understanding coming from the heart that holds an unshakeable belief in students' ability to achieve and in their (the counselor's) ability to assist in that achievement. Talk about time (arrival and departure) and absences. Avoid hiring someone who might want to come in at 7:00 a.m. and leave at 3:00 p.m. and take no lunch. Once, when the time issue was never discussed in the interview, the counselor arrived at 7:00 a.m. No administrator was as yet present. Her argument was "others come that early and leave early and don't take lunch."

Avoid happenings such as this by clarifying everything you can possibly think of at the initial interview. Don't assume anything. Assumptions differ from person to person.

Motto: *Getting to know you—getting to know all about you.*

Savvy Strategy 53: Use Staff Meetings as an Inclusionary Tool

Most schools have a full staff meeting at least once a month. These are usually conducted by the principal who uses them to bring the staff up to speed on, or make them aware of, certain happenings relevant to the business of the school. The agenda is most often developed by the principal with input from staff, district headquarters, etc. It would be helpful if the counselor was solicited for input into the agenda. The form of the input could include such items as:

1. Current research on psychological concerns of students (age relevant to those enrolled in that school)
2. Parent concerns (all generalized—no names)
3. Counseling goals (e.g., working toward improving reading scores through parent groups)
4. New secretary in counseling office—introduced
5. Referral forms (where located and how to access)
6. Feedback forms (where located and how to access)
7. Update on progress toward school goals, etc.—by the counseling department

Counselors can list concerns or discuss them here, but they should not turn these meetings into complaint sessions. The main purpose of inclusion in these meetings is just that—that they, the counselors, will be seen as part of the school team—working toward mutually acceptable goals. Often teachers see the counselor as someone students go to—if they're in trouble, need a class change, need a referral, need help in college selection, etc.—but don't see them as part of the overall school team.

Counselors are part of the team—an important part, and as the school's team leader, you, the principal, can foster that concept in a very overt way by including them in the meetings, arranging for their items to be addressed, manifesting interest in their reports, and modeling the overt respect and interest you wish the rest of the staff to have in counselors as well as in each other. In addition, by not feeling that counselors are apart and perhaps less important or relevant as they, staff will be more ready to use the services available to them that you are paying for out of your overall budget.

Motto: *All for one and one for all.*

Savvy Strategy 54: Have a Formal First Meeting

After the counselor has been hired, or if they've just been hired and they're already in place, or if it's the beginning of a new school year and you've both been working together for a while, have a formal first meeting of

The New School Year
The New Hire
The New Arrival

It's always good to clarify, reclarify, verbalize, or reverbalize rules and expectations. Commit or recommit—change or add. This is an important step.

Be sure the staff member clearly understands your expectations. It's been frequently found that this is an area in which misunderstandings thrive. Counselors will say, "Oh, she doesn't think that's important; doesn't care about that; really is concerned about something else, etc.," and their misunderstanding couldn't be further from the truth. The first meeting should make clear that you appreciate their profession and expect certain things from them.

This is the time to talk again about attendance and punctuality, reports, records, assignments, dress, and the schedule of future meetings. It would be very helpful to have these items written out, and maybe ask the counselor to sign for having received this listing. Some principals delegate this task to their secretary or assistant (would John Wooden not have an opening session with a new hire?). There's really no substitute for *the boss*.

Jack Welch, former CEO of GE, tells the story of requesting a meeting with source managers of specific units under him (Welsh, 394). These positions were often held by not-so-perfect men. When their managers heard whom they were meeting with (the boss), they "nearly died," and they were often replaced with more effective staff. It all had to do with the importance of meeting with "the boss."

At this time you should set up a schedule of (1) when you'll meet again during the year; (2) what you'll be doing to help the program along; (3) what you want right away; and (4) what you're hoping to have happen in the future.

You're the main cheerleader for this person, this program, this school—if you're paying for this service out of your budget you should expect it to produce. You'll get that production more readily if you keep looking for it and let it be known that you are looking for it. Don't belabor this meeting; Rome wasn't built in one day. Leave some things to be discussed at future scheduled meetings. This meeting should be the supportive kickoff.

A few major ground rules can be discussed; things that you especially want to happen—being on time, good attendance, schedule of whereabouts known, etc. And focus on the school's major goal and assurances of your support and hope for success.

Motto: *You're the leader of the pack.*

Savvy Strategy 55: Do Your Homework (Office, Mission Statement)

Be sure you know if this person has an office, or a place in which to work. On one occasion a counselor at the elementary school level, having met with the principal, was told that Ms. X, the morning kindergarten teacher in Room 11, would show him where his office was located. Approaching Ms. X's room, he discovered Ms. X was absent, her replacement had no idea where the counselor was to go, and the principal had just left for a meeting. A bad start. The counselor felt abandoned; the principal, when he heard about it, felt embarrassed, and the staff internalized the idea that this wasn't a very important addition to the staff if no real provision had been made for his first day.

The "office," incidentally, was to be a little closet off of the kindergarten classroom, which Ms. X used to "coach" afternoon students and her partner used in the morning to coach morning students from Ms. X's class. Think about the yearly salary of this counselor and how much productivity can be gleaned from it when a person is limited to such quarters.

Yes, counselors "make do" and achieve some really good things even when hampered by such constraints, but how much more could be done if their time and skill were used primarily toward counseling and school goals and not always trying to find a place to function? Your support and guidance in the area of office location, placement, setup, furniture, supplies, etc., is invaluable.

If you have a capable assistant principal, perhaps this can be effectively delegated, but as Harry Truman is quoted as having said, "The buck stops here." This is an important component that must be addressed. People feel very territorial about space allotment. Teachers, especially at the elementary level, have been called "kings of their castles" and are often reluctant to give up any part of their castles—even a portion of the closet—and would you want to talk to a counselor in a closet?

Students are very perceptive, also. Being relegated to a closet to discuss something of real importance to them might very readily defeat the purpose of providing them with help and support. The boiler room, cafeteria corner, and front office desk may often fall into the same place of rejection. Be creative—when pushed custodians have become inventive and quite capable of providing more than adequate additional office space.

By showing you care enough to place this "diamond" (your counselor) in a setting as close to Tiffany-like as possible, you're protecting your investment (the cost of their wages) and helping to ensure the success of their efforts.

Further homework should be devoted to the knowledge of who is responsible for the ongoing training and coaching of this person.

As principal, you are responsible for improving the "quality of instruction" at your school—in addition to selected areas of administration. But what about the further training of the counselor's professional discipline of counseling? To whom does a counselor turn for the training and coaching needed to improve?

As principal, most likely you have not been trained as a counselor. Does your district office provide ongoing staff development for counselors? Are the counselors members of professional organizations that will provide for that training? Do the local universities (if there are any) have staff that would be willing to serve as coaches and/or guides to counselors? Would the local universities offer group discussion groups for counselors, in which counselors could meet on a regular basis to discuss concerns and share successes?

What about volunteer services of retired counselors (hopefully ones of which you have positive memories) to mentor individual counselors—to help them along the way? Many districts have access to state and county office personnel who possess a great deal of expertise in these areas. If necessary you might have to go through district channels to access these people, but if your district sees that your feelings are serious about the importance of a good counseling program, they might be happy to provide access—or provide it themselves.

Setting a person in an office, checking on them every so often, and providing necessary supplies and motivation is important, but ongoing enrichment and nurturing of their skill development to be sure they are current with the most recent techniques and procedures is vital.

Motto: *Be it ever so humble . . . but hopefully not that humble.*

Savvy Strategy 56: Schedule Counseling Staff Development Meetings for the Entire Staff

Include the staff in what's happening in the counselor's office. In order for staff to see the counselor as a true part of the school team, they should be aware of what goes on in the counseling office. A full staff meeting at least once a year should be devoted to counseling and counseling procedures and staff involvement—with time at the end for questions and concerns. Particulars relevant to counselor's hours; responsibilities; referral sheets; participation in overall school goals; and procedures with students, parents, and services to teachers should be discussed and the method of feedback to staff should be explained.

A brief skit can be arranged depicting students' concerns or actions when in the counseling office. A counselor's technique of straight information giving or Rogerian or Adlerian method of helping a student arrive at his own answers, the guiding of a parent to accept the reality of student's present ability while realistically helping him or her to improve, the coaching of a student for a summer job interview or camping trip—all of these instances will give staff greater insight and understanding of the counselor's role and how they might best use this service.

The importance of selected procedures for counselors to use when providing feedback to staff should be thoroughly discussed, and the topic of confidentiality in counseling should be explained both from legal aspects and the general professional aspects. This is the place in which the professionalism of both teaching and counseling should be stressed. If mutual respect is to be achieved, it is here in these general staff development meetings where both sides acknowledge the value and dignity of one another.

It is important that the principal be there—all during the meeting—to overtly manifest interest, concern, and endorsement for the counseling discipline, and by their very presence they underscore support and encouragement for these team members and the desire that staff support and avail themselves of these services.

The teaching staff should be made aware of any changes, student concerns, latest research, and new methods of operation as well as being reminded at least annually of procedures already existing to assist them in assessing, addressing, and surmounting all barriers to student achievement. Counselors should be able to provide a program regarding their discipline that will be enlightening, enriching, even perhaps entertaining, but certainly illuminating to their fellow staff members—and the principal will have made it all happen.

Motto: *We're all in this together.*

Savvy Strategy 57: Have a Counselor as Part of Your Advisory Team

Every principal has, or should have, his or her own advisory team. This is the team that addresses school goals, plans strategies, analyzes evaluation results, and revises activities in light of those evaluations. This is the team that's comprised of staff members dedicated to achieving positive results in light of the whole child, in light of whatever barriers to learning might exist, and in light of the needs of all participants in the process. This is the team that definitely needs representation from the counseling office.

It is most important that counselors be aware of the total picture of school life. So often they are relegated toward dealing with students who have major problems in school and are on the fringes, so to speak, of school activities. By being aware of and understanding the total picture of the school's needs and concerns, counselors can help guide and direct these "fringe" students toward more positive participation in school life (if they're not aware of what this life is, how can they direct students toward it?).

In addition, by facilitating staff awareness of the needs, concerns, and failings of the aforementioned "fringe" students, counselors can perhaps facilitate other staff in the ways and means of providing easier access for these students back into mainstream school life. For example, staff was concerned with procedures for emergency exit drills developed for crisis-time happenings. The drills were not being conducted in a timely manner. The delays were often traced to selected students with certain behavioral problems who were also counselees of the resident counselor.

After a discussion by the principal's advisory council, counselor input suggested a buddy system, whereby other students immediately sought out selected students assigned to them and helped these students leave school quickly and safely. One counselor also was able to include this topic in regular counseling sessions with students, helping them develop insights into the necessity for and importance of quickness in these drills.

Counselors were not expected to betray any confidences at these meetings but were expected to share general impressions of overall attitudes and moods. Other advisory staff personnel were expected to share concerns and happenings relative to their own areas of professional expertise. These meetings set the tone for the value construct of the school.

The tone of cooperation most often is set by the school principal. It is a major job, and principals need all the help they can get. A good place to start is with the advisory team.

Motto: *Hearing what you think can help shape what I do.*

Savvy Strategy 58: Share Information: Counselor Must Be Included in What the Principal Knows about Student(s), School, Future, etc.

Oftentimes a student is referred to the counselor by the principal, "This child has problems; This child needs to talk with you; This parent could benefit, I think, by meeting with you." Principals often refer people to the counselor and give little or no hint as to what they expect to have happen, what the cause of the referral might be, and what, if anything, might be discussed in a counseling session. The referred student or parent or even teacher might state, "I don't know why she wants me to see you. I have no idea what's going on."

It's difficult for the counselor to demand a proper referral slip from you, the principal—so valuable time is lost trying to identify the problem—and then perhaps it's not the specific problem about which one is concerned. Communicate, communicate, communicate with this staff member. Tell her or him exactly what's going on and why counseling service is being requested for this particular person.

In addition, be sure to share information relevant to school matters with the counselor; for example, if budget cuts are being discussed and rumors are flying—clear the air with facts. If the police have told you of a ring of whatever illegal activity you can name is suspected of being in the school, or the school is on a list indicating it might close—share this information—not for the counselor to publicize, that's your job—but for the counselor to understand why certain anxiety seems to exist within the staff or with parents or students and be prepared to deal with it.

Counselors, too, should be willing to share information of a general sense, such as students' anxiety over impending tests, students' fear that a certain teacher might be leaving, etc., so that principals might more readily understand their student body and react accordingly. Let it be understood that we're not talking about a tattling situation here. The counselor is not the principal's stooge, nor vice versa. We're talking about a team that is constantly sharing the pulse rate of the institution.

No counselor confidentiality is to be broken. Counselors are not to share specifics about a specific person—but overall atmosphere and pending trends seen from meetings, discussions, and observations. Seeing the counselor as a *partner*, not an informer, might help to clarify this procedure. Seeing one's principal as a fellow soldier in this struggle for the best student, best school, etc., should formulate how this process can work best.

Keeping secrets is a malfunction of personal power. Sharing information is a manifestation of machinelike perfection.

Motto: *The truth, the whole truth, and nothing but the truth.*

Savvy Strategy 59: Express Approval of Counselor's Area of Expertise

Try very hard to compliment this person at least once a week. (That means you're going to have to see them!) Notice what they're doing; notice the faces of those who leave their sessions. Be aware of their relationships with other staff members. Are teachers referring students to them—do they turn to them with concerns about handling students?

Is the counseling office occupied with clients, or is the counselor more often than not in there alone, reading or writing or talking on the telephone? Those last three activities are necessary, but not to the exclusion (for the most part) of the interactions with clients that is the backbone of the counseling process.

When the positive aspects of counseling are observed, take a moment to compliment the counselor. When a positive remark relative to their service is heard, share it with them.

Many counselors feel that the only time the principal speaks to them is to state something negative (e.g., "With money so tight positions like yours might be cut next year," or "Another student on suspension? That's all that seems to be happening lately."). This is being said to the person that's supposed to be one's left arm! It's like beating that arm with a stick and expecting it to function better. Express approval of their reports, feedback, willingness to go that extra mile to contact parents, secure job interviews for students or older siblings or even the parents themselves; securing speakers for staff development programs, etc.

An unpublished survey conducted some years ago, "A Penny for Your Thoughts" (Los Angeles County Office of Education), indicated that principal and staff approval ranked high in a counselor's list of items that make them feel pleased in their jobs. Asking their assistance in areas where you feel they should have expertise goes a long way toward validating their self-worth. Areas might include such topics as learning styles of selected children, therapeutic techniques for dealing with issues of bereavement, and the latest statistics and research on childhood and adolescent depression and suicide.

The school counselor, as a result of their training, will most likely have a wealth of information on these topics. By turning to them for this and similar information, one is validating that specific knowledge and also motivating that person to continue to enhance their learning and understanding of these relevant areas. Even if they don't have the answers immediately, most likely they will know how to go about getting them, *and* in the meantime they will be flattered and positively impressed that the school leader reached out to *them*.

To keep the school institution running like a well-oiled machine is a big job. In order to do that one has to be aware of and tend to all parts of the machinery—noting carefully that they're running well and providing whatever it takes to keep them running well. Nurture, encourage, support—if something untoward happens and it must be addressed also, do so—but do it in the context of all the other positive things, not as if this negative happening stood alone.

Set the benchmark high—underscore its existence repeatedly so that should a negative occur, it will stand out clearly and be obliterated swiftly.

Motto: *Hearing "well done" makes one feel second to none.*

Savvy Strategy 60: Spend Some Time in Their Office

Take an opportunity to visit the "turf" of the counselor. Get a feel of the comfort level of a visitor to that site. How would you feel being there as a parent, a teacher, a student—all these could and should be clients of the counselor at one time or another. How do you feel as an adult, as a principal, going there? Are there pictures, slogans, a comfortable seat? What about privacy (at least audio)? Is the place too stark, too messy, too cold, too warm, too little air? Where does the counselor sit in relation to you? Do they seem relaxed? Does the phone ring constantly? Do people burst in unannounced? If you ask him to look for a student's record, is it locatable in a reasonable period of time? Is there a record?

Visiting someone's office manifests many things—that you feel an interest in what's going on there, that you're a hands-on administrator, that you're a team player–type, not a top-down authority figure, etc. Of course, a great deal also depends on what the counselor is feeling, also. They might perceive the visit as a "checking-up" type of activity—something conducted to find fault, an intrusion, a violation of confidentiality.

Of course, one doesn't burst in on a counseling session unless a major emergency is happening. You may even wish to schedule the visit; for example, "I'd like to talk with you about test anxiety that seems to be increasing. Suppose I stop by your office tomorrow at 2:15 p.m.?" Or you may be passing by and just pop in, "Are you very busy, can you spare a few minutes?" Whatever way you do it—do it. The important thing is to be familiar with all venues of service under your control. How can you in good conscious support them, change them, enhance or eliminate them—if you don't know them?

Before the visit, be sure you have a goal—observation of the physical setup, discussion of a particular topic, information regarding specific learning patterns, etc. Pop-in visits for the sake of "having been there" are just that—place markers on a checklist of things to do. Principals do many things, their time is valuable, and they are in the most important business of all—developing the minds and attitudes of future generations.

Motto: *Knowing your turf is like tending your garden.*

Savvy Strategy 61: Invite a Counselor to Sit in on Selected Conferences with Parents

By including the counselor in conferences with a parent, you're validating their expertise in this area—not only to the counselor but also to parents and others on the school staff. This is so important in terms of empowerment, confidence, and sense of belonging—as well as learning. It also imparts the message that it's important to seek out others who might be of help. So often, educators feel they must do it all alone, make all decisions by themselves, demonstrate that they are in possession of all knowledge, and never ask for help or recognize expertise in others.

Counselors are often called upon to deal with acting-out children—only to find the cause of the acting out to be a lack of reading or math ability—resulting in behavior problems in that class! What a boon to dealing with this problem to have the reading or math teacher part of the counseling session to help deal with remedial or tutorial strategies in that particular area.

The inclusion of a teacher in a counseling session would, of course, only be done with the permission of the student and after the counselor felt that a basic relationship and bonding with the student had taken place. The principal, too, might also request a parent's consent to including the counselor in his or her meetings with parents. Extending courtesies and being courteous at all times is mandatory for establishing a civilized society. And where better for such establishment to begin but in school?

Having the counselor sit in on your meetings also demonstrates your willingness to be observed in the performance of your duties. It is no small thing, and it is excellent groundwork should you request to sit in or be an invited guest at one of the counselor's activities (e.g., orientation meetings for new students, group guidance meetings on the importance of homework, attendance, promptness, etc.). Of course, your attendance at these noncounseling activities (as opposed to those in which confidentiality is involved) doesn't really require consent, but it does give a nice tone to it! It should also be noted that your presence at the above-described events always gives an added importance to them—something that counselors always find most helpful.

Having the counselor attend parent conferences that you've set up is also good public relations with parents for using the counseling service. If it is seen that the head of the school feels this service will be helpful to them, then the likelihood of their using the service will tend to increase, and that's all to your advantage. It frees you up for other chores and indicates to parents that your school has the facilities for dealing with many and various problems. It also provides you with the perfect opportunity for observing your counselor in action.

Are they able to establish rapport with the parents in your office? Are they able to assess the problem, offer strategies and suggestions for the evaluation of goals and follow-up? Have they left out an important step? You're right there to observe, assist, and assess and provide feedback at a debriefing. So open your door and invite in a valued team member.

Motto: *Discussions and training are important, but observing "in action" is vital.*

Savvy Strategy 62: Be as Involved as You Can Be

Let it be known from the beginning that you intend to be involved in this program—not overriding but positively supporting the assistant principal for guidance. State to the counselor(s) that you feel this program has a great deal to offer the school, and you want to help make it happen. State your awareness of how counseling is an integral part of the functioning of the school and, whereas selected curriculum areas have the focus at this time for evaluation and achievement, you see counseling as an important part of arriving at that achievement goal.

In addition, you may state that, as a permanent part of the school budget, counseling is fully recognized as vital to the life of the school, the achievement of its goals, and as a remover of many of the current barriers to learning.

With these stated feelings regarding the importance of counseling (which you might wish to have published in the school newspaper) you can then reinforce the idea that you intend to be involved in the counseling efforts as much as time will allow. You may wish to state that such involvement would take the form of:

1. Review of weekly tally sheets regarding counselor activities (you may wish to review tally sheet forms to be sure activities in which you feel counselors should engage are included).
2. Sitting in on certain nonconfidentiality-requiring activities (e.g., orientation meetings, classroom group guidance sessions).
3. Requesting the counselor's participation in open-school nights.
4. Reviewing counselor daily program sheets.
5. Office drop-ins (during noncounseling times).
6. Other activities that you feel would provide you with a greater understanding of the program and how it is working to meet school goals.

This is something for you to do and not delegate. Yes, there are many things to be delegated to assistants and others, but overall involvement in a vital component is not one of them. See yourself as the director of this movie—concerned with its greatness, concerned with all aspects of its moving parts.

Motto: *Actions speak louder than words.*

Savvy Strategy 63: Share Budget Information

Perhaps this should be the first item dealt with as principals attempt to carve out their role in dealing with counselors. Often, but not always, counselors have little or no idea of how the school budget evolves, how it is developed, adjusted, grows, or compresses. Some counselors will say "That's not my job," some will say, "I could really use a new computer," or "I'd like to go to that conference," or "With my case load we really need another half-time person."

Show counselors how their services are provided for; what is expected as a result of paying for such services; and asking for needs input, such as books (reference), paper, pencils, computers, secretarial time, conference attendance, space, facilities, etc. Such knowledge should enable counselors to gain a better picture of their place and part in the overall structure and workings of the school.

Programs can be geared to alleviate ills and increase revenues. One such counseling program in San Diego, California, geared to improving attendance, demonstrated how ADA (average daily attendance—rate on which school funding is computed) was increased sufficiently to cover counselor salaries. Another program had similar positive results by decreasing graffiti and school vandalism, thereby freeing up amounts that had been budgeted for them for use in other ways, which demonstrates school counseling effectiveness.

By sharing budget information with counselors, asking for information regarding their needs so those needs might be budgeted for, and requesting counselors' thinking on how their services might be used to assist in budgeting strategies (see above), you have the opportunity of getting skilled input displayed in monetary ways.

In addition, do not negate the possibility of additional funding through counselor contacts in the world of grants. Counselors have abundant knowledge regarding local, state, and federal funding sources—often gleaned from colleagues. Camping scholarships, intern programs, and special books for fun and scholarships, all provided by private grants, have often been identified by counselors—especially when asked by an involved principal to help in this regard. What a stimulus to creativity!

As an added note—don't forget to include any largess of this type on your overall report to the district office. Clearly, it will show how successful your efforts have been in developing an outstanding counseling program.

Motto: *Show them the money.*

Savvy Strategy 64: Take to Administration Meeting(s)

This might require some planning on your part and permission from district or county personnel (whichever educational subdivision in which your school is located), but it will go a long way to underscoring your support for your counseling program and strengthening your counselor(s) feeling of team work.

Principals usually meet at least once a month with the district superintendent. At these meetings budget matters, educational codes, new laws, new curriculum approaches, testing results, and state and federal requirements in different areas are frequently discussed—all topics of importance to educators engaged in the administration of schools.

Hearing firsthand about budgets, new programs, new laws, etc., could be most meaningful to counseling staff. Seeing firsthand how principals must wrestle with these difficult techniques and procedures allows for empathy and respect to develop and strengthen. If confidentiality is required due to the delicate nature of certain selected issues at these administrative meetings, counselors should be made aware of such and agree to act accordingly.

On the other hand, you might wish to have your counselor report to the district on some successful techniques they have developed or used in their offices that might be replicated and shared with other schools. This type of recognition is appreciated and perceived most gratefully. Communication, inclusion, and involvement enhance us all. Show you care and respect others' abilities. It pays off in great dividends. Other school administrators can benefit from the sharing of successful practices.

Success is more often than not achieved as a result of teamwork. Unfortunately, counselors often do not see themselves as part of the team. A major manifestation of a strong team is the sharing of activities and experiences. Meeting attendance of this type is an activity and experience that should help greatly in this regard.

One might have to tread carefully here in regard to the role of the assistant principal. They should not be made to feel usurped or excluded, but they should definitely be included in all these counselor-enhancing activities.

Motto: *A view from the top usually entrances the viewer.*

Savvy Strategy 65: Provide Time and Funds for Their Attendance at Professional Development Meetings

Budget funding should be made available for counselors to maintain their professional growth by attending workshops and seminars geared toward helping them keep abreast of current trends and the latest developments. Such workshops or seminars should be structured around topics both of interest to the counselor *and* focused toward achieving school-stated goals.

General conferences and keynote sessions are helpful, but it should be noted if within these usually large conferences certain topics are included that specifically address needs and goals already identified as being relevant to your school. The principal might readily select said seminars, having identified them from advanced program guides.

However, it is more likely that such meetings will be identified by the counselor. When this occurs, be sure to require a written request for attendance along with a written explanation of why such attendance will be relevant to the counselor and helpful toward enhancing the school goals. Allowing the attending counselor to report back to the staff (five to eight minutes) about this meeting is usually very rewarding. If longer information is needed by the staff, a written report could be handed out. Either way, a written report should be on file.

Meetings and the sharing and learning of new ideas are important. So often, the final step of reporting back or putting ideas into practice is lost in the press of everyday happenings. A good leader does not let this occur. If you show that you think what happens at professional development seminars is important, others will think likewise. Furthermore, if you feel that what you got back in terms of information, the activity of an improved program, improved counseling practices, etc., did not warrant future expense of this type, discuss this with the counselor and make future decisions accordingly.

In addition, during the counselor's absence for professional development training you may wish to consider hiring substitute or retired counselors to cover some of the counseling duties. Perhaps there is a cadre of retired counselors who would be willing to provide this service on a volunteer basis. Seeking task replacement personnel is another way to underscore the feeling that the counseling staff is vital and important to the functioning of the school.

This business of seminar/conference attendance has always been a "bone" of contention in all schools. By tightening up on the "raison d'être" and providing outside personnel for the absent counselor, you will be bringing this issue better into line. By also showing the counselor how this is included in and impacts the counseling budget, you should be well on your way toward getting your dollar's worth.

Motto: *Where are you going, what are you doing, how will it help us?*

Savvy Strategy 66: Support Your Head Counselors

Can you fantasize that in a large school district in which head counselor jobs brought a new title, a larger office, a substantial raise, and additional clerical support, among other "perks," these jobs went begging? It has happened. Head counselors have reported that the job is too difficult.

The main reason for this difficulty is lack of support from the building principal. It's important to provide that support and assistance. The power flows from you. Noting that you support your middle-management person, others will also. Be involved here. Request minutes of head counselor's meetings with staff. This will give you an excellent idea of what's happening in this area and a clue to what the identified needs of this group might be.

The head counselor is in the administrative circle. His or her major task is to run the counseling office. He or she must deal directly with budgets, materials, personnel, personality issues, competency issues, space issues, etc. Your help is needed! One head counselor reported that her principal told her to get rid of a staff member who wasn't producing but didn't give her any specific pointers other than what the general handbook stated. All the while the principal kept complimenting the nonproducing staff member and smiling kindly at her.

The head counselor involved did all she could, wrote out the situation clearly, took the report to the principal for review, and was told, "Be sure you get her keys when she leaves." The issue was finally resolved with help from the district personnel department. However, nerves were stretched thin, and transfer requests were tendered. There is no need for this to happen if there is understanding and support. Maybe there was a hidden agenda in this case, but as a rule, captains should help and guide lieutenants or wars can be lost.

Motto: *Be protective of those who serve as your right arm.*

Savvy Strategy 67: Be Aware of Duty Assignments

Counselors perform a variety of activities in order to achieve stated goals, such as telephoning and attendance counter work (questioning of students arriving late and issuing them passes to attend class; checking parental notes after a day or more of absence, etc.). Hopefully, students understand these changing "roles" and adjust accordingly, for these types of activities can be seen as being included under the counseling "umbrella."

It is not so easy a task when the counselor is shifted to straight disciplinary-type activities (yard duty, lunchroom duty, hall duty, perimeter duty [checking to see if students might have left the campus, if campus had been closed during lunch, and all other student activities]). These types of activities appear to fit more readily under the school discipline "umbrella," rather than the counseling one.

Counselors participating in these activities must oftentimes assume a different attitude and manner than that of mentor, guide, confidant, and counselor. Students, ever perceptive to attitudinal changes in adults, might very well see this as a betrayal of some type, and the main task of the counselor would become more difficult and less effective.

In order to know and understand these situations better, counselors may often take on the role of observer, visiting school yards, lunchrooms, perimeters, etc. However, as an observer they are not in a position to enforce rules, dole out punishments, or report infractions. This is not to say that in their major role they might not discuss their observations with students in order to help them deal in a more positive fashion with particular issues.

Principals should be aware of all tasks in which counselors engage in order to meet their objectives. They should also be aware of possible deleterious effects certain assignments can have on counselors' relationships with students, and if possible forgo the possibility of assigning such tasks to the counselor.

Attendance at school activities (plays, football games, award ceremonies, etc.) are events at which counselors can observe student behavior and perceive student relationships with peers (and possibly parents and faculty advisors). Being aware of the counselor's activity schedule (this should be posted on their office door/Internet and initially approved by their immediate supervisor) and respecting it—by not interrupting with meeting requests or other types of summonses—will go a long way toward underscoring your endorsement of their activities. If on occasion you should have to interrupt some activity, be sure to apologize. Simple courtesies are golden reinforcers of respect and approval.

Motto: *To divide can sometimes defeat the overall goal.*

Savvy Strategy 68: Share Counselor Efforts as Part of the Total School Plan

Can you imagine your feelings if the district superintendent left your school's test scores out of the district report of written district school test scores? Or left your name off the alphabetical listing of district principals, or even listed the wrong address for your school? Even if the mishap was apologized for, or laughingly explained, down deep you might readily feel a certain degree of unimportance, of insignificance, of failure.

You might even begin to question if this was not a "sign" that your efforts were unimportant in the total scheme, unnecessary to the overall picture—a Freudian slip? Certainly this would not be a positive occurrence and would not be something you would like repeated.

Being "left out" at some time is something we have all experienced, and on occasion we have withdrawn our willingness for future participation. By formally including *counseling* in your monthly reporting format, not just as a separate entity but as an actual variable to be positively considered when striving toward overall goals, you will reinforce the importance of the discipline.

This reinforcement will take place not only in the minds of counselors but also in the other members of the educational team. This recognition of counselor value will go a long way toward providing the soil for continued and expanded growth and development.

One of the major duties of a school principal as is often stated is "to improve the quality of instruction." In the course of pursuing that duty you may wish to include recommendations to a classroom teacher, such as "You may wish to discuss strategies for helping student improve focus with the counselor" or "You may wish to review student's attendance problems with the counselor and ways for improving same." By including counselor recommendations in teacher's observation reports (when appropriate), you will be underscoring the role of the counselor's efforts in the overall school plan and encouraging teaming.

By including counseling as an active component in the school plan model you highlight the role of the service and encourage activities by the counseling staff. You are also encouraging utilization of the counseling service by others within the school compound. When efforts are noted, stated, and examined they tend to cause the producers of such efforts to feel more relevant and more motivated to improve—even on what might be considered a job well done.

Motto: *Inclusion is often a better motivator than exclusion.*

Savvy Strategy 69: Make the Counselor Aware of Your Goals regarding Counseling

Humphrey Bogart's famous line, "Here's looking at you, Kid," has never been beaten over the years as the ultimate quote of attraction, support, attention, and endorsement. He did not say, "Here's to ignoring you, Kid, and letting you do your own thing" or "I don't know what you did, Kid, but I'm sure it will be fine." No, he said, "Here's looking at you"—not just here's to you, but here's looking at you.

People might say they want to be let alone to do their own thing without interference, but the large majority want to be recognized and encouraged, even critiqued—if it is done without malice—along the way. If you are really committed to improving the counseling program at your school and have taken it on as a personal goal for the year or even the quarter, let the counselor know. Tell them that you feel they and their professional discipline have a lot to offer the school, and you are going to be looking at this service with new ideas—seeing how it can enhance the goals of the school.

You may wish to share any particular insights you are aware of that have shown the importance of counseling (several have been cited in this book) and state that you feel such results might be replicated in your school. You might wish to use this conversation to ask the counselor if he or she knows of any specific way you could be of assistance to them in the improvement of the service, the greater utilization of the service, and the furthering of specific guidance techniques and procedures.

Try not to open the door to complaints or gripes. Try to keep this to a statement of intent to put counseling and the counselor on the radar—an intent to recognize, support, and endorse; an intent to look at with love. This should not be an "I'm putting you on notice" type of conversation, but a conversation indicating the dawn of a new era. The launching, if you will, of an inclusionary effort of a service that might have been overlooked in the past.

Giving some indication of how this inclusion might take place could very well note some of the very issues already discussed in this book. When it is clearly understood that logs and reports will be included in district reports, when the effect of efforts will be measured in connection with budgetary contingencies, when service is seen as an important variable to the total educational plan, and when skills are recognized as vital to producing a really good product (an educated student/citizen), the counselor should and most likely will feel further motivated, encouraged, and supported.

Don't approach this effort in a clandestine manner. Announce, launch, and proclaim, "I'm especially interested in this service and will be focused on its greater development ("Here's looking at you, Kid.")."

Motto: *Communicate, clarify, compliment.*

Savvy Strategy 70: Suggest or Join a District or Superintendent's Committee regarding Counseling

Why try to reinvent the wheel? Your colleagues are a fount of information on many topics. Most likely they have had pet projects and have many strategies readily available for enhancing them. There might be in existence already a districtwide, statewide professional association type of committee geared specifically to this issue. If one is not readily at hand you might want to start one: The Principals' Committee to Enhance School Counseling and Guidance.

The point here is to support your efforts and reach your goal faster by not trying to travel the road alone. In addition, by joining, starting, or asking questions relevant to this issue you are sending a clear signal regarding your interest and concern. Of course, there can be a political, personal, or professional problem with such an action. "Is he trying to start up something to curry or gain favor or attention; does he want to focus attention on this service for personal reasons; is the program in her school so poor that she needs help or so exceptional that she wants to show it off?" These issues can surface in the minds of some, but if presented carefully and with a diplomatic attitude that bespeaks seeking to improve a student's lot in life, then concerns can be ameliorated (or let's hope so!).

Before you suggest the formation of such a committee, it would be helpful to write out clearly stated goals for such a body—as you see them. So often committees can be set up on a name-only basis (e.g., the retreat committee, the financial committee, even [dare I say it] the curriculum committee). Such committees most likely have been in place for years, and members have a preconceived idea of what these units are all about.

When establishing a new committee or requesting one, do some preliminary groundwork. List goals you might want to reach, such as:

- awareness of successful programs
- acceptable ratios of counselors to clients
- funding sources available inside and outside the district

- volunteer services available
- existing and new laws regarding this discipline
- method(s) of determining success
- identifying the particular needs of each school within the district (or the district as a whole) that might be met through the counseling program
- bullying prevention
- how counselors might assist principals in meeting their goals, etc.

Have suggestions available for possible meeting sites and times and perhaps an agenda outline for the first session. Outlines should call for *much* input from members—selection of a chair and the developing of future agendas along with a suggested date for a final meeting and the date for reporting back to the superintendent and/or the group as a whole.

Having this material ready will help you have your thoughts in order, but this must be presented carefully. Perhaps it even should be edited down to "We might have a committee to look at counseling programs for the purpose of getting the best out of these services. I'd be willing to host the first one at my school." It would be a good thing to give a "heads up" regarding this to the district pupil services director so that person doesn't become anxious about or feel blindsided by your efforts.

If it has been known (and things travel quickly in districts) that you've been a supporter of counseling and guidance, this type of request will probably not be unexpected. However, floating the "trial committee" balloon suggestion takes a certain degree of courage and bravery in a group that's probably overburdened to begin with.

Be prepared for some negativity. The timing of the suggestion is important, and if at first you don't succeed—at least the seeds have been sewn and they very well might blossom at a later, more fortuitous, date.

Good luck.

Motto: *One is often known by the committee he forms.*

Savvy Strategy 71: Request Minutes of Counselor Meetings to Ascertain Needs

Often head counselors will hold meetings of the counselors within their school (your school!). These meetings should contain an agenda that shows that planning has taken place and a summary of what is discussed and decided along with any future assignments, dates, etc. By asking your head counselor for copies of these minutes you show concern, interest, and involvement.

At times principals might feel that the head counselor might see this as being intrusive; a form of checking up or spying. Steps can be taken to prevent such feelings by saying how important you feel the discipline of counseling to be, how much you want to be involved in its success, and how minutes of meetings help you readily assess concerns and needs. If the head counselor's anxiety persists, perhaps this is a major indication of the necessity of your involvement.

If the school does not have a head counselor, but only one counselor on staff, you might ask to see the minutes of any district or state meeting the counselor attends, mainly for the same reasons: to ascertain needs and concerns and to be aware of future happenings in that area. We are all cognizant of the plethora of meetings that educators attend; closing the loop by asking for meeting reports is often a forgotten step in helping the profession move forward. In terms of a principal who is dedicated to supporting a particular feature of the overall school service, getting minutes or reports of meetings attended can be a major factor.

Let's face it—even with the increased dependence on the computer we are still also a paper-and-pencil profession. Ask for a printed-out copy of the meeting report from the head counselor or counselor, as the case may be. Take a few minutes to review, discuss, and comment on the meeting. Hopefully, the bonds of support and encouragement will be strengthened, your understanding increased, and your overall program improvement achieved. And isn't that what it's all about?

In addition, there's an excellent chance that the quality or productivity of those meetings will improve—probably by a meaningful degree—for when a meeting chair or leader knows that someone is reviewing meeting minutes (as opposed to having them just filed) a desire for greater effectiveness is born. When one knows one's efforts are being observed, those efforts take on a greater energy. So, by simply monitoring minutes, reports, etc., you will most likely improve them. Sounds like a sure bet!

Motto: *Monitoring, checking, reading, improving—all in a day's work.*

Savvy Strategy 72: Provide Cadre of Retired Counselors for Emergency Times

More and more the regular counselor is being called upon to provide specialized services during times of emergency. I am referring here to grief counseling, suicide prevention, child abuse prevention, terrorism concerns, and other types of necessary reactions to specific happenings. What happens to the regular tasks of the counselor—such as class changes, ongoing support in a behavior situation, parent meetings dealing with obesity, etc.—and teacher conferences regarding obstreperous students when the regular counselor is pulled out to provide those specialized services?

To put the regular counseling duties on hold can throw programs out of gear, as the day to day running of the school labels these services as unimportant and confuses and upsets counseling clients. School administrators have at times called for auxiliary services (trauma centers' staff, counselors in private practice, etc.) to handle the emergency situation. That has been helpful, but oftentimes students, staff, and others seeking these services wish only to speak with counselors who are permanently assigned to their school and who are aware on a firsthand basis of exactly what has happened.

Insurance issues can also be of concern in these instances. On these occasions it is helpful to have at one's disposal a cadre of credentialed counseling personnel who can handle the everyday duties and tasks of the school counselor. Credentialed counselors, retired from your school or from the district or living in the area, might readily be identified beforehand and surveyed regarding their willingness to assist in this regard.

Funds might also be set aside beforehand to address such emergencies. Questions regarding volunteerism could also be entertained and discussed. Organizations such as district, city, and state school guidance associations could be contacted regarding the availability of personnel to form such a cadre. Such efforts on your part will clearly indicate superb managerial skills for dealing with crises along with an understanding of the importance of preparedness.

Your knowledge of the importance, relevance, and place of counseling in emergency settings as well as the daily business of the school will have been clearly demonstrated along with your respect and admiration for those who have gone before. The on-staff counselor will have demonstrated proof of your feelings regarding the need for her discipline, and the school community will appreciate your concern for the importance of carrying on in the time of difficult happenings. Having a backup team always at the ready is the sign of a strong and valiant leader. Hoping you'll never have to call on them is the prayer of every current leader.

It might also be helpful to list the names and titles of this cadre of retired staff (for example, "credentialed school counselor") in any district or school brochure that identifies school personnel.

Motto: *Old counselors never die—don't allow them to fade away.*

Savvy Strategy 73: Listen

We give no awards for this and yet so many, many of us want it! When we ask others about their day, we'll often say, "How's it going?" The expected answer—O.K. or great or so-so. Some people often answer, "It's gone." All these answers usually elicit from us a smile, a nod, a one-word comment—"Fine," "Great," "Right." But rarely do we stop still after that and wait. Just listening, showing by that listening that we are interested, that we're there, that we're attending. No, our goal is not to serve as a therapist or counselor. Our goal is to show interest, support, concern.

This is about getting the best services for the school to which we have been assigned as principal. In order to do that, it's important that we shore up and support those staff members assigned to provide those services. Counselors have often stated that receiving support from their principal really helped them, made them feel like a valued member of the team, and enabled them to do a better job. Having access to you is part of feeling appreciated. Being listened to is another part of being supported.

Listening means paying attention, and it comes with a whole set of characteristics. As a principal, you've learned to be a multitasker, and you can *hear* what someone is saying when you're doing something else—but perhaps while you're *hearing*, the speaker doesn't think you're *listening*. Two different words.

Years ago during a cooperative review on the guidance program in a small school district in New York State, the students were discussing what made for a good counselor in their school and remarked that "counselors had to listen." "Surely, they all do," the reviewer remarked. "No," said one student. "How can you tell?" asked the reviewer. "If they're writing while we're talking, they're not listening." Interesting, for surely, the counselors in that district and all other districts hear what students say and act on what they hear and provide assistance for students in terms of what they hear—but support perhaps also comes from the feeling that one is being listened to and that they are being clearly heard.

As a principal trying to support a program, *listen* to the staff member—project the support that listening entails, let the staffer know that although you're very busy that you are concerned, that you are there for them listening and willing them to succeed.

Realizing that they are being listened to by the most important person, the main person in their school, is a major ego boost, and with it comes a feeling of strength and security that will encourage and provide support for their efforts. Counselors have often felt alone in their efforts to assist in the educational achievement of students through their particular discipline. By listening attentively and completely to them you are making an overt manifestation of their place as a part of the educational team. It's needed, it's wanted, and it will pay great dividends.

Motto: *A good listener is a silent flatterer.*

Savvy Strategy 74: Publish

Nothing seduces educators like the published article. In the towers of higher learning the expression "publish or perish" is often mentioned in relation to job retention or advancement for the professional staff. There's something about seeing your words or facts in print, ascribed to you, that usually enhances you and lets others understand, accept, and hopefully applaud your views. In addition, by having your words on a topic formally put forth you're letting it be known, for all to see, your exact feelings—pro or con—relative to a topic.

If you have a strong feeling relative to the support of the counseling program in your school, having your words published in an article relative to this in an educational journal or magazine will be a very big boost, first of all, to the counselor(s) involved in that program.

Secondly, school staff, district staff, and others in the immediate proximity to your school will read it—often just because it was you who wrote it—and will become more aware of this positive service.

And thirdly—members of the entire educational community will have an opportunity to hear about a successful program or practice that they might be willing to replicate in their own setting. The article might well be submitted to the district bulletin, the state or national guidance journals, and/or the multiple journals and magazines targeted especially for principals, administrators, or general education readers. What about local newspapers, also?

As educators we are constantly on the alert for "things that work," and how better to learn about them than by hearing about them from a working principal who wants to move his or her school ahead? Certainly, psychologists and counselors can write and talk about their programs, but it's sometimes looked upon as in-house discussions.

Words of support from a principal relative to an in-action program are viewed in a different manner and by a larger audience. You can easily obtain a listing of journals and magazines that would be appropriate for your article from your school or district librarian.

Think outside the box and perhaps submit the article to the local or city-wide newspaper or to the local radio or TV reporter or TV show host who reports on successful projects. (A note to the wise here—it is good policy and protocol to run all articles prior to submission by your superintendent's office or district public information office for approval.)

Think about all the ads and notices you see promoting movies, Broadway plays, new novels, political calendars, products, etc. People like to know what's out there. People are aware of endorsements and endorsers. People buy more advertised products than unadvertised products. People can't use, can't replicate, can't support what they don't know about.

If you really believe in this service, help support it and those involved in it by writing about it and talking about it when you can. In these times of budgetary concerns let's be sure that educational funders don't redline a marvelous service because they didn't know about it and no one spoke up for it.

Motto: *When all else is gone, the written word remains.*

Savvy Strategy 75: Support Emotional Intelligence

As a principal, your main role as it is so often defined is to support instruction, curriculum, and achievement, and that is a most laudable objective. However, the overall goal of the whole system of schooling is to provide an understanding for students as to the ways and means by which they can use those skills learned in class to become worthwhile and productive citizens of the society in which they live—to further benefit themselves and that society.

In his book *Emotional Intelligence: Why It Can Matter More Than I.Q.*, Daniel Goleman explores this topic at length. He cites examples indicating over and over that pure intellectual knowledge is not sufficient to provide for success, productivity, and happiness. He highlights the importance of anger control and impulse control and notes five major characteristics and abilities of emotional intelligence.

1. Self-Awareness—Understanding your emotions and being able to identify them when they occur.
2. Mood Management—The ability to handle your feelings through proper control and reaction.
3. Self-Motivation—The ability to rise above feelings of doubt, depression, and inertia to move forward toward a goal.
4. Managing Relationships—The ability to get along with others and handle conflicts in an acceptable manner.

5. Empathy—The ability to understand the feelings of others, being in tune with the variety of ways these feelings may be communicated to you.

Confidence, curiosity, intentionality, self-control, relatedness, capacity to communicate, ability to cooperate—have been looked upon as key ingredients in the understanding of how to learn and are noted as critical elements for a student's success in school (National Center for Clinical Infant Programs Report). These traits are aspects of emotional intelligence and are all traits we hope to develop in students today. However, with the heavy aspect of preparing students to do well on standardized tests, teachers have little or no time to focus on these other aspects of learning.

This could be an important role for the counselor. By providing pathways into the curriculum for these traits by reviewing the existing "method of instruction" in the various curriculum areas, perhaps avenues for these traits might be given a gateway. How many times have we heard our teachers say to students, "Control yourself." Perhaps by providing steps and procedures for so doing and doing effectively we could be laying an important foundation for future learning and taking less time out of the process to say, "Control yourself," since students will have learned how.

By supporting exploration of this topic and supporting ways and means by which it can enhance the quality of instruction we, as principals, will be giving the nod to the area of expertise of our counseling staff.

By having them become more aware of this area, attend seminars on this topic, report to the staff on its ramifications, and demonstrate how aspects of it can be woven into everyday classroom instruction, we will be accomplishing a duality of goals—first to enhance the understanding and awareness of current research in brain-based studies concerning emotional health and effective learning and secondly to outwardly manifest our own endorsement of the importance of our counselor colleagues.

The overall benefit of this is to the students, who will gain the necessary emotional skills to deal more effectively with and succeed in life.

Motto: *The river of intelligence can have many tributaries.*

Savvy Strategy 76: Support Bibliotherapy

Since we're discussing your major role as improving the quality of instruction and the making of students who will become good and productive citizens, let's not forget reading! Reading—one of the mainstays of our curriculum—is surely high on your list of areas to be enhanced, nurtured, and improved upon. Reading for knowledge, reading for enjoyment, reading to improve the quality of one's life.

Books have often been used in the counseling office to help young people further understand certain problems, issues, and situations confronting them. Reading about these issues sometimes in factual texts but more often in fictionalized accounts helps students realize they're not the first to confront certain problems—that others have done so, gotten help, often emerged successfully, but have always been able to move on.

Books have been an invaluable tool for counselors to use with students to help increase understanding, provide language for discussion, and showcase practices and procedures for dealing with life happenings. Students today are bombarded through the media, Internet, text messages, movies, magazines, peers, and games with occurrences that we often feel are adverse to our desires for them. How wonderful to have an effective practice of our own to counter this bombardment.

Principals should encourage counselors to use this practice and be aware of the many books available to them for this activity. By including monies in the school budget above and beyond the basic counseling budget you are directing, endorsing, and encouraging a practice that has had proven results in many instances.

Most recently Tara Parker-Pope reported in the *New York Times* on a new series of books, described as the "Beacon Street Girls focusing on real issues like popularity, weight problems, alcohol, and divorce." Her report highlighted a study from Duke University presented at the annual Obesity Society's scientific conference. The study noted some dramatic results related to desired weight loss obtained by selected girls who had read the book *Lake Rescue* (B*tween Productions 2005), one of the Beacon Street Girls books that focused on weight loss, as opposed to others in the study who had not read the book.

Having books available to students that will help them better understand some of the difficulties they are facing as well as providing trained personnel to discuss this material with them can go a long way toward helping students with particular problems occurring in the now and providing them with a positive strategy for dealing with problems in the future. As a principal, assuring counselors of available monies to purchase such materials shows strategy leadership, professional support, and administrative respect for their discipline. It is not up to you to identify the books to be bought, but it is up to you to set a tone of acceptance and encouragement for successful practices.

Reading, as we know, in elementary and middle schools is a most important curriculum area. By combining reading and an approach to positive mental health and physical well-being you are setting a tone and climate for a win-win situation. Even if the results hoped for from the book's content are not immediately achieved, at least seeds have been sown and literacy promoted.

Motto: *Something is learned every time a book is opened.*

Savvy Strategy 77: Be Sure They're Part of a Team

When there is only one counselor in a school, a major complaint has often been that they feel very lonely, apart, and have no one with whom to share concerns or successes. No one who understands their discipline, their role in the movie! Surely, as principal you've reached out and included them in meetings, conferences, etc. However, the areas in which it's been suggested that they be included are primarily your areas.

We are now suggesting that they be included in the basic school area. Over the years counselors have been teamed with psychologists and social workers in a variety of programs. One of the earliest programs of this type, the Early Identification Program (EIP, circa 1959) occurred in selected New York City elementary schools and identified elementary school children at the second-grade level beginning to manifest discipline and learning problems at school. Once identified, the team sought ways and means for dealing with or ameliorating these problems and assisting students at this crucial period in life.

The team of counselor, social worker, and psychologist had the opportunity of learning from one another, appreciating one another's efforts, and gaining combined respect for their disciplines from parents and staff. Combinations of school nurses, counselors, and physical education teachers could also be considered to address some of the health challenges facing students today.

The fact of the lack of student achievement in areas of science might lend itself toward a combination of counselor, science curriculum specialist, and scientific community worker being brought together to address this concern.

Certainly the current state of the global economy is ripe for counselors teaming with specialists in these academic areas and the general community. If you can include your counselors in these various areas of immediate need in your school community you are saying to them that you respect and admire what they have to offer and that they are *needed* to make your projects successful. You are also saying to others that you—the most important person in the school—value your counselor's expertise and you are modeling the attitude you wish others might emulate.

If important committees are established and again and again counseling staff are excluded from participation, then they are viewed as apart from a school's major issues and as having little or nothing to offer. If, on the other hand, their contributions are sought out on certain matters then they will be respected and sought out on other occasions by those who have observed this, and you will have promoted the use of a *valuable* and *costly* service that might otherwise have been grossly underused.

Our world is so often about costs and use of valuable resources. This book is about helping you get the most out of your costly and valuable resource—the school counselor.

Motto: *We all have the same goals. Let's work together to achieve them.*

Savvy Strategy 78: Remember to Motivate

On the television show *60 Minutes* (May 25, 2008), it was reported that the motivation industry is a $50 billion-a-year business. Top industry leaders are spending all this money to encourage staff to do better, to be more productive. Industry leaders also want to discover what things really motivate their people.

In education we talk constantly about motivating our students—what can we do to make them score higher on tests; control their obstreperous behavior; complete homework assignments; follow rules. What about motivating staff? Salaries are often established by district and union negotiations, and merit bonuses are delicate issues. More often than not salaries are out of individual principal's hands—so the financial aspect of motivation is most likely beyond your control.

However, as has been previously mentioned, in an unpublished study conducted years ago, counselors indicated that they felt mostly motivated by statements of approval from staff and administrators. Can you recall the last time you complimented a counselor on a specific achievement? Can you recall a specific achievement requested of or achieved by a counselor?

More often than not, counselors are looked upon as those who "keep the lid on," so to speak. No rumblings, no upset parents, no disruptive students, no complaining teachers, no issues for administration to react to—just status quo from the counseling department.

This is not to say that a calm, noncomplaining, compliant student body and teacher/parent cohort is not to be appreciated (but it's difficult to say "you're great—no one's complained about anything today").

In *Success Built to Last* (Wharton School Publishing 2006) Jerry Porras, Stewart Emery, and Mark Thompson prefer to refer to successful people as "builders" (it is difficult to feel like a builder when your main job is keeping the lid on). These authors write that builders find success when three major elements come into alignment in their lives and work:

1. What you do must matter deeply to you.
2. You must possess "a highly developed sense of accountability, passion, and responsible optimism."
3. You must "find effective ways to take action."

As a principal, just sitting down for a half hour to share these elements with your counselor(s), discuss them in a general sense, and set a time in the future (one or two months) to revisit the topic could go a long way toward motivating the group.

Hearing these points, knowing you're looking at their efforts, and realizing a follow-up has been planned should help counselors feel valued, and feeling valued is a major part of being motivated. Motivation means moving on—not staying still, not just surviving. Of course, in some cases today, just surviving, holding fast, staying the course can feel like a considerable achievement. However, it is not building, and in order to feel successful, one must feel like they're builders—careful accountability can show that certain buildinglike achievements have been made. Help your people see this, congratulate them on it, and push them to the next level.

By encouraging your counselors to find new, more effective ways of doing things, you will not only be motivating them and helping them to feel more successful, you will, according to Nancy Kalish, who writes in *Prevention*, be increasing their brain power. "Your brain is a thrill seeker," Kalish writes. "New experiences stimulate the area that produces dopamine, a chemical involved in learning and memory. Studies show that doing new things builds brain mass and increases mental agility."

Motto: *Words of encouragement can spur the heart to heights.*

Savvy Strategy 79: Focus Each Day (The Power of Five)

The turning around or moving ahead or the moving to a stellar position of the counseling component of your school is not just a brief line in your to-do diary. If it's going to work, if it's going to make a difference, it needs focus, attention, and daily commitment on a renewable basis.

Having a little card on your bedside (yes, bedside, not office) table saying, "Did I help the counseling program yesterday? How can I help them (it) today?" will help you start your focus early enough that it won't get sidetracked. You've committed to this, and you're building something that will have a personal payoff and a far-reaching one in terms of children's lives and the future of those of the next generation. What can be more important than that?

Ask the counseling staff to do this also. Suggest to them the process of focusing on one good thing (that they've achieved for a student/parent/teacher program or have made happen in the face of defeating odds, or identified as a new, more successful way of handling an old problem) each day and listing that item.

Elaborate by asking them to share this listing with you (five items for five days—or a school week). Explain that you won't be asking for these every day, or every week, but intermittently, unannounced. Ask that they be written down. You will be helping this staff focus on positives, on achievement, on problems solved. You will also be able to note the complainer, the staff member who sees this as just another task, who doesn't care to change, who likes operating beneath the radar (as if you didn't know). However, often if you can snare them into this activity, a spark may ignite and a not-too-hopeless cynic might be changed into an amazing achiever (and that's what we call HOPE).

By focusing yourself each day, you're also providing the brain with the stimulus it needs to bring about the achievement you want. The brain is motivated to seek resources to answer its questions. By keeping the question in the forefront, by questioning achievement accountability, by asking yourself what you did each day—have you been successful?—you're actually prodding the brain to develop more answers. By doing this around bedtime or upon rising you're allowing the brain rest-time intervention to provide you with resources. By having yourself focus on how you moved toward your goal each day, you're focusing more and more on success; soon, soon, it will be yours.

Motto: *Positive focus every day keeps you pointed in the right direction.*

Savvy Strategy 80: Are They Modeling You? (Who Are They Modeling?)

Everyone needs a role model. We always seem to be looking for one. "Who are your heroes?," we ask children. Who do you want to be when you grow up? What behaviors of *yours* would you want your staff to follow? How you dress? How you speak? How prepared you are for meetings? How innovative you are? How good a follower you are—of directives, policies, authority figures? How professional you are? How serious you are? How courteous you are? How fair you are?

Are you aware of what characteristics you display? Are they the ones you wish to display? How would you like others to see you? Do you think they do see you that way? Have you ever done an anonymous survey—asking hard questions about your performance? Do you want to—do you think it matters? Do you feel it would do more harm than good? Do you ask for suggestions from staff, students, and parents relative to what they might wish to have happen? What characteristics would you want to see prevalent on the part of staff? Are they your characteristics? Are you showing by your actions how you expect staff to act?

A good leader often leads by example. Have you been setting the example you want others to emulate? Do you want your staff to act as you do, or simply follow your directions? Are you then following the directions of others, and if in so doing things go awry, whose fault is it anyway? If you want to know where counselors are at all times so that they can be called upon readily when needed, can you be reached at all times? Do you keep all appointments as scheduled, or are some more important than others?

Leadership is tricky, but the characteristics of a strong leader are often quickly emulated. The tale, often told, to exemplify this for young teachers is of the teacher who frequently rubbed the lobe of her right ear. By the end of the week two of her pupils were doing likewise. Percentages grew as time went on, until by the end of the semester most of the class was given to rubbing their right ear lobes at least two or three times a day. A leader is one whose people follow. Be sure you are leading by your example in the way you want your people to follow.

If there are certain reports you wish from your counselors, share a glance at a report you might have just finished for your superintendent. If you feel they must learn to be calmer in the face of an angry parent, share a look at the tiny, black, ceramic cat on your desk that you've learned to stroke when you're under certain pressure. Share some of the selective techniques and procedures you've amassed to help your staff along the way to designated goals.

The title *principal* originally meant the main or principal teacher in the school. By this modeling for your staff you will continue to be that main teacher.

Motto: *A good leader is followed willingly.*

Savvy Strategy 81: Highlight Importance of "Mothering" (Promoting Students' Mothers!)

It seems our athletic coaches are way ahead of our academics in recognizing the importance of mothers in young people's lives. The sports columns often feature how coaches will often court and woo mothers of prospective candidates for positions on college football teams. A warm story in the *New York Times* on January 25, 2009, gave the account of Jamarkus McFarland, a star football player of Lufkin High School in Lufkin, Texas, and his final choice to attend Oklahoma State University because of the positive impression their coaches had made on his mother and grandmother!

These coaches had won over McFarland's mother especially with their kindness, consistency, courtliness, and manners. Winning over the mother had won over the son. Other universities had tried gallantly—offering many inducements—but in the end, winning over the mother had done it all.

Another player's story (by Karen Crowley, *New York Times*, September 30, 2007, Sports Sunday) tells of the hope of Jets player David Barrett, whose mother left her three children with a babysitter and never returned home. The case was still open twenty-eight years later. David was too young to remember his mother but still hopes for her return. The *Times* article quotes him as saying, "I missed never having that person you can come home to and call mom, who will put her arms around you, and tell you she loves you."

Mothers play an important role in their children's lives—as parents should. By taking the leadership role here, underscoring this fact and perhaps suggesting that they move on this to effect better academic learning and social behavior of students, you may be providing counselors with a vital success component.

On a recent television program of *Meet The Press* (January 11, 2009), Maxine Waters, congresswoman from Los Angeles, California, proposed the idea of a parenting component as a special part of the curriculum. This component is not presented by teachers or added to their academic subject matter burdens, but it is one spearheaded by another section of the academic community. What a great role for counselors!

Perri Klass, MD (author of *Making Room for Miss Manners Is a Parenting Basic*) says a lack of good manners and social skills in children can impact their physical health and should be a concern of their physicians and a definite part of the parent role. Counselors might really spearhead such a project involving mothers!

Schools across the nation either have established or are beginning to establish "deportment" type groups, such as Carver Elementary School in

Compton, California. These groups at Carver are called Young Ladies of Unity, and its counterpart is the Gentlemen's Scholar Club. These are wonderful ways for students to adapt to society. *Parents should be involved in this project, and counselors could readily lead the way.* Principals, pointing out these happenings, supporting these efforts, and encouraging counselors to address this variable are more likely to have successful projects than just allowing the project to happen by chance.

As principal, your focus on including parents as cooperatives in reaching stated counselor goals can go a long way toward encouraging counselors to include this valuable resource in their work process. I realize that you're walking a line here when it comes to the counseling process, but the fact is, it's your school, and the outcomes for the student's achievement ultimately rest with you. The buck stops with you. By indicating your awareness of the importance of and preference for the inclusion of parents (when possible) in the counseling program, you are providing the leadership that comes with your office and your title. You are the boss. Go for it!

Motto: M *is for the million ways . . .*

Savvy Strategy 82: Have Interim Evaluation/Progress Assessment Meeting(s)

Early on in the suggestions to principals for improving the counseling program in their school, it was recommended to have a formal first meeting. A getting to know you, getting to know me meeting, this is what I can do, this is what I want done, etc., meeting. Oftentimes this is the only time principals, especially high school principals, have such a formal meeting with the counselor(s). Elementary school principals do meet more frequently with counselors, but the meetings are usually informal.

It might be suggested that a series of at least two meetings a year (more would be better) are scheduled—a folder established by the principal, notes taken, and progress toward stated goals assessed. Principals may assess formally or informally, e.g., "discipline doesn't seem to be getting any better," "fewer students seem to be accepted in four-year colleges," "teachers do not seem to be referring students to you for counseling support," etc.—or student evaluations of counseling services that are quite positive—three mothers' groups were held over the past semester; student involvement in outside voluntary aid groups is up; etc.

It is supposed that all areas mentioned above were stated and listed as goals of the counseling program. By having a list of stated goals and having a time when progress toward those goals is noted and discussed gives a kind of structuring support to the program. In addition, by having the principal address this issue—take formal note of it, have an ongoing folder where this information is maintained—underscores the importance of the activity in the eyes of the activities' participants. It also indicates the program's value and worth.

Think about those clothes kept back in the closet—year in and year out—without wearing them. They were important when we first bought them, but as time moves on we move them to the back of the closet, rarely looking at them and never wearing them any more—interesting that the *New York Times* Style Section on May 14, 2009, has an article regarding "Treasures in the Back of the Closet" and discusses how in these times of budgetary concerns and stringencies we should search out these "treasures," look them over, redo them perhaps to meet current trends, and profit greatly by the *attention* given to these overlooked items.

Perhaps counselors have been feeling pushed to the back of the closet in these days of high-tech and standardized test scores focusing mainly on mainstream curriculum, and this taken-for-granted group might do well with some rediscovering and updating. Unfortunately, as the main cheerleader and director of the school, you the principal must address this task. Delegating to an assistant or chair and then meeting only with that person is okay as far as it goes. However, hands-on leadership means just that, hands on. You have to meet with the troops. You have to have your own folder showing that it's your gathered information—your concern, your interest.

Methods of evaluation should be agreed upon at the beginning of the year. Self-assessment is nonthreatening and easily understood and undertaken. Student, parent, and teacher assessments of service may be a bit more threatening and might be piloted first with a small group of students, teachers, and/or parents. You may wish to include the special questions from Jeffrey Krames's book *Jack Welsh and Leadership* that asks, "What do I as a manager do to hinder your efforts?"

You might simply review tallies: number of students seen, parent conferences held, classroom guidance lessons given, counselor development classes attended, etc. The important factor here is attention—your attention to the discipline of counseling. This "treasure" should not be relegated to the back of your closet. As educational budgets tighten, every resource must be used to the fullest to produce the golden gems that are our children of the future. Helping to guide them to those days of promise is the role of a lifetime, and that role is yours.

Motto: *Always know how it's really going.*

Savvy Strategy 83: Be Aware of Occurrences in a Counselor's Personal Life

A horrifying crash in Buffalo of a commuter plane in 2009 highlights the importance of supervisorial awareness of personal happenings in subordinates' lives. It appears that one of the pilots was ill with a cold and sore throat and had only a few hours sleep, had been working an extra job, and apparently had not been fully trained, while the other pilot had repeatedly failed certain required courses for his job.

Airline administrators appear to be arguing that adults should be able to monitor their own lives, assess their own capabilities, assess their own skills and readiness to work, and carry out their own assigned tasks. Does the administrative staff have no responsibility in this matter? Who's in charge here—the administrator or the worker? This is often an issue to address as principals.

Perhaps it behooves administrators to know if counseling staff is ready to counsel or if some personal stress may be taking its toll and rendering them less than able to give their best. There are many listings of the multiple stresses facing adults today. (T. H. Holmes and R. H. Rahe allocate units to varying stresses or life crises and suggest a score that might possibly incapacitate a person.)

Such crisis as a death in the family, suicide of a friend or loved one, divorce, job loss, moving, new baby, caretaking of an elderly relative, etc., can take a psychic toll and physical toll on an individual. As an administrator you may readily expect the effects of this situation—this happening may spill over into the counselor's work product and effort. It may even affect their attendance, and substitute staff may have to be employed.

Awareness of happenings in a person's personal life also allows administrators the opportunity to provide personal support to the staff member—a kind word, a show of concern, a supportive gesture or action can go a long way toward helping a colleague and alleviating a situation. Most people do not want to feel that they exist alone in a noncaring world. Principals, on occasion, have stated that they do not want to appear prying into staff lives or have to take on the role of "father confessor" or life coach to staff.

Let's look at this carefully. As principal your job is to improve the quality of instruction and student outcomes in your school. Most of the hands-on work with students is done by staff (like the pilots on the plane that have to get the plane to the destination while the company administrators manage this effort), while the administrator manages the total effort! By being aware of the well-being of staff, attending as well as possible to their stresses, you are operating in the realm of your assigned role. This may necessitate acting as father confessor (until you can wean them on to a more professional type). Usually, this type of situation is short-lived, but your understanding, support, concern, and attention is long-lived in the awareness of your staff member. They know they're in a nurturing environment, and as such they will gain strength and flourish and you will reap many benefits as an administrator, and more importantly, as a human being.

To paraphrase an old saying, "When you do not have hope, you look for it in the face of your friend." By bringing someone who is undergoing a life stress back to a world of hope, you are a true educator leading one out of darkness into light.

Motto: *Two most powerful words—"I care"—use them!*

Savvy Strategy 84: "It's Always Been Done That Way" (Support Necessary Changes)

You've heard it many times at school, at home, at the bank, car shop, etc. Watch out for this phrase; it can be a showstopper, and it doesn't even have to be set to music. And there are many variations on this theme—such as we've always done it this way, or we tried that and it didn't work, or nobody wants to go there, do it that way, has the time for that. Staff may readily admit that times have changed, students have changed, customs have changed, but methods, goals, and tasks of personnel must remain the same.

A classic tale is often told about Ichabod Crane, the schoolmaster in New York State who fell asleep for one hundred years and when he awoke he walked about and saw giant buildings where there had only been open fields when he had fallen asleep. He saw four-lane highways with motor-driven vehicles on them where there had only been dirt roads for horse-driven carriages. He saw flying machines over his head carrying people, and he was very frightened and couldn't internalize the changes he was witnessing. He began to tremble, and his fear grew.

"Where can I go?," he thought. "Where can I run to feel safe and secure?," he asked himself. And then he thought, "I'll go to the school house. Nothing will have changed there. It will all be the same." And he was right.

Perhaps we have been slow to change, but we are definitely picking up speed, and as principal you don't want your counseling offices to be left behind. Surely the computers and Internet access are available and established, but what about the other technological accoutrements that have surfaced of late? Cell phones, texting, video games, digital cameras, recording pens, and the psychological ramifications connected with the rampant technology—in many schools and with many students and their families, these issues are of major concern.

This is a relatively new area of involvement—perhaps you wish your counseling staff to be brought up to speed in this regard. This will then call for some staff development training in order to have quality work rendered—not just "flying by the seat of my pants" service. *Ask* them if they are prepared to handle these issues, and if the answer is in the affirmative, ask about their training.

Perhaps the area of new technology is not a major concern at this time in your school. Then, make certain that the particular goals you have determined are those on the front burner. Perhaps this is the time you're focusing on discipline, or on academic achievement, or on career-track students. Don't be swayed by the "we've never done it that way" people. Hold fast to your goals, and by so doing you will ensure that the counselors will hold fast to the new goals that have been set. The familiar, the tried and true, is seductive, and it has been successful in the past in many instances. Perhaps it is not necessary to change. If not, then don't. "If it ain't broke, don't fix it."

However, be sure it's your choice not to change. *You* are the *principal*. You are the one where the buck stops. This doesn't mean you're a dictator. Listen, of course, to all constituents, but *you* must make the final decision. And do not be afraid to try or to fail. You will learn from every action—if nothing more than not to do it that way again for now. But, if you have a vision of success, a vision of your way bringing the type of staff and counselor achievements you want, then by all means go ahead, and don't be swayed by naysayers.

There are barriers to learning out there that can and should be removed by counseling staff. Issues involving gangs, gender identity, the autism spectrum, family economic catastrophes, incarcerated parents, etc.—issues that perhaps were not addressed in the past but that can severely impact a student's ability to achieve in school.

These new issues will need a new methodology of approach, and our efforts to address them and help our clients (parents, teachers, students) to address them cannot be impeded by phraseology maintaining "we can only do it this way."

Motto: *Embracing change can make it a friend, not an enemy.*

Savvy Strategy 85: Clarify Your Motive(s) for Involvement

Sooner or later your counselor or counseling staff will begin to wonder, "Why is there so much interest in us?" So perhaps you might wish to have this dialogue or discussion early in the school year. I would also suggest that it not be a one-time activity. Remember, your role here is that of the major success motivator. You're pushing something you very much believe in, and for a myriad of reasons. Sharing some of those reasons with the counseling staff can be very beneficial.

Certainly, in these days of economic stringencies it's important to ensure that all monies spent under the education budget are used wisely and well. That having been said, you might wish to acknowledge the fact of what a benefit a good counseling staff can be to the academic and career life, and in many instances the personal life, of a student.

Anecdotal reports from elementary school students having counselors available to them at that level showed that they thought more highly of the service and used it more at the middle school level than students not having such services available in elementary school. Anecdotal reports from students and parents have often praised counselor efforts—indicating how fortunate they were to have the counselors available to them at crucial turning points in life.

As a principal you, of course, want this type of service available for the student body in your school. Perhaps your highlighted involvement at this time could be the fact that you are wanting to turn a failing or mediocre school around and want to use *all* assets in this quest or, as one principal told his staff, he had a bet going with a principal colleague that he could raise his average reading scores by one grade level, and he was pulling out all the stops to do it!

Another principal told his counselors that he was turning to his guidance staff because he had come up through the counseling ranks and knew the many abilities and strengths that resided in counseling staffs and wanted to publicize those strengths and abilities.

Personal challenges, altruistic motives, the desire for new experiences, involvements ("I really never knew much about your field, I was a math/science teacher") whatever—share a reason for the interest. One would expect that this group that is in reality very capable and stretched very thin would respond very positively to your interest. Think about why you picked up this book and "blue sky" a bit about what a "perfect" counseling staff might accomplish—how you might best help them and feel comfortable that you will achieve all that and then some.

Motto: *Explaining can be difficult, but done well it can pay dividends.*

Savvy Strategy 86: Patience

You have embarked on a very special effort, one that can be difficult to achieve. Oftentimes it's in your mind's eye exactly what it is you want to achieve. Sometimes the picture is clear, and at other times it's cloudy, with many gray areas. You need help on this journey, and one of the most valuable tools is patience. Of course, you'd like everything to be achieved in one day. Since the invention of instant coffee we've become a nation (we probably were one before that) of people who want everything accomplished *instantly*!

Gifted high school students in Budapest just after the fall of communism were having a conversation with a visiting educator from the United States. When complimented on the fact that they spoke English quite well, they stated that they didn't like the way they spoke English at all. "We want to speak with an American accent," they complained. "Why?" they were asked. "We want to speak with force and say things like, 'We want it and we want it *NOW*, just like the Americans talk.'" A clear picture of us? Perhaps. Like most things in life, this can be good and not so good.

As a principal, wanting things NOW can perhaps set you and your staff up for major disappointments. On the other hand waiting too long for things to happen can also bring about defeat. It's good to have a big goal and maybe little goals along the way whereby to judge progress—to let you know you're moving in the right direction.

A major academic goal of every student advancing a year on standardized math achievement tests might have smaller goals of having at least 75 percent of all students being present every day for math class; 80 percent having the text with them, 80 percent having some homework with them, 60 percent having completed homework, and 40 percent having all homework assignments completed and correct. Depending on where you're coming from, the baby goals will vary. (Getting to Los Angeles by plane may be a major goal, but getting there from London is probably going to take longer than getting there from Phoenix—it sort of depends on where you're coming from!)

Patience can be important for you as principal, but it's also important that you are able to impart it to your staff. Sometimes they can become very disheartened that their efforts are not bearing the fruit that they had expected. Counseling staff members might wish very much to meet the hoped-for stated expectations of you, the principal. If this doesn't happen almost immediately, they can become disappointed, embarrassed, ashamed, and depressed. Be there for them. Compliment them on their efforts—point out small successes, suggest other benchmarks, examine the situation to determine factors that might be impinging on success and elements that might be added to ensure or at least strengthen the possibility of moving ahead faster.

This also might be the time to reexamine the major goal. Is it truly realizable? List all the assets you have for achieving the goal as well as all the obstacles (real or imagined) that are in the path of goal achievement (when *all* the planes are grounded, you may have to go by car, train, and/or boat!).

Time magazine of February 25, 2008, page 31, cited a National Center for Educational Statistics report that the top reasons teachers cited for leaving the profession in 2001 was the *lack of time to prepare*. Such a response might readily be admitted by counselors who have caseloads of students of over three thousand in some high schools (Manual Arts High School, Los Angeles, California, reported such in *LA Magazine*, September 2008). Trying to be prepared for each student as they approach their appointments can be a Herculean task and often very disheartening.

Time seems to go on forever—but situations and people are finite. Learn to blend these factors. Don't let a lack of patience on your part doom the entire project. Use a prop to open another window for success and happiness.

Motto: *Rome wasn't built in a day.*

Savvy Strategy 87: Integrate Ideas— Take from Academic and Use in Counseling

Consider some of the successful programs in the academic areas and tailor them for use with counselors. Take a look at the merit pay plans being put forth—some individual, some advocating performance-based pay on a schoolwide basis. It's very hard to argue against rewarding someone for a job well done, but there have been arguments in our field of education for a long time. The reverse can take place. When some counselors were not up to par, a whole program was dropped and the good were let go with the not very good. This isn't easy, but you might want to explore it if you're up to forging new paths!

An especially successful program for teachers was developed in 1999 by the Milken Family Foundation and is now in over 180 schools in fourteen states. It's called the Teacher Advancement Program (TAP), and it has some strong advocates. It also has a career-ladder type of aspect whereby teachers can advance by staying in the classroom and becoming master teachers, becoming mentors, or by moving into administration.

This might be adjusted to a ladder program for counselors. TAP calls for regular meetings two hours each week with a master educator. At these meetings goals must be articulated, strategies planned, supervisorial visits arranged, and reflections written on how well lessons went. This model might be easily adjusted for counselors.

Counselors work so often all alone, and rarely, if ever, get the opportunity to discuss how things went in student counseling, group counseling, teacher guidance, or parent interview sessions. Yes, of course, there is the question of confidentiality, but this could be handled by the No Names rule or other strategies. The important consideration is for an opportunity to question and consider and reflect and learn from others under the guidance of a master.

The idea of a career path is a good one, also. There are those who may want to remain as counselors, others who may wish to move on to administration, and still others wanting to become master counselors who impart their skills to new counselors and colleagues.

Foundations like Milken and others have often expressed deep support for the advancement of education programs that are geared toward the helping of students to advance academically. Being able to show these foundations about how school counseling is an important component in that regard might enable you, the school principal, to secure the funding necessary to enhance your counseling program and provide the enrichment desired to make a good program become a great program.

Motto: *No tunnel vision allowed!*

Savvy Strategy 88: Bring in the Stars

In this day and age many of us are "star" struck. We are often focused on those that are the leading proponents in a particular area—sports, film, music, etc. A counselor/administrator, when asked what she felt her principal might have done to help her improve her services as a counselor, responded immediately, "Bring in the stars." "Show us how the experts did what we were supposed to do." "Or," she continued, "If *anyone* could do what we were supposed to do."

She went on to indicate that curriculum experts were often on hand to explain new teaching techniques but rarely, if ever, were such steps taken to afford counselors the opportunity to broaden their skills and services. When she became an administrator, she continued, she tried to remedy this situation by contacting universities, county and state education departments, counselor professional organizations, and staff themselves to identify these experts and make an effort to bring them to the campus.

Funding and other factors can often make this difficult. It might be necessary to send counselors to the larger professional organization conferences to see these experts and hear them speak. Such practices need follow-up by the home administrator, such as written reports of the presentation, discussion, and demonstration of the learning at the school level. Videotaping of these sessions is also an option, as is video participation in actual demonstration lessons. It can happen, but it takes administrative direction. In high schools, there is often a head counselor or assistant principal who can spearhead this effort very effectively, and often does.

However, such efforts do not negate the importance of the chief school officer—you, the principal, from *visibly* supporting, endorsing, and monitoring the effectiveness of this happening. You would not divorce yourself or be apart from the efforts of the assistant administrator in charge of curriculum who was bringing in a curriculum "star" to enhance teacher efforts in math—thereby showing your belief in the importance of math.

It is the same with guidance and counseling. Yours is indeed the bully pulpit in the school. When you show your endorsement for an area it goes a long way toward having others provide their endorsement, also.

There are new and important happenings and strategies going on today in the area of counseling and guidance. There is a high school in a difficult area in the Bronx, New York, where the students have not been scoring in the high percentiles and many financial constraints have impacted parents. The high school counselor there took it upon herself with the motivation of the principal to secure college placement for *all* graduating seniors, and she has achieved her goal. The *Wall Street Journal* has written about this counselor of All Hallows High School in the Bronx, and she might be willing to speak at your school or professional organization, if contacted.

The relatively new concept/technique of "mindfulness" has been successful in helping students focus better and achieve more. It has had some surprisingly positive effects on depression also and could be a technique most helpful to students at the middle and high school level. Jan Kabat is noted as the "star" of this effort, and Dr. Jim Hopper has workshops available to counselors and might be willing to visit the school.

The above examples of recent happenings in the field are indicative of the "star" areas that could lend themselves to staff learning and duplication. Also be aware of "stars" closer to home, successful counseling programs that exist in your city or state. Keep your mind open to these occurrences and share them with counseling staff and, if possible, bring these "stars" to your site or arrange for staff to learn from them in some way or another.

And what about the "stars" you might have identified in the counseling department of your own school? Make sure they get some good press, and be willing to allow them to share their formulas for success.

Motto: *When in doubt look to the heavens.*

Savvy Strategy 89: What about Discipline

If one talks with educators for any length of time (often in the first few minutes) the topic of "discipline" will often arise. It may be expressed as "classroom management," "group control," or some other euphemism, but it's about discipline. As the school principal you, too, are concerned with discipline. It's often linked with safety and also with learning and achievement. Counselors, especially at the elementary school level, have also been linked with discipline. Many times, the school principal has charged the counselor with maintaining "discipline" in the lunchroom, the hall, the school yard. On many occasions, counselors have often complained that all they do is "discipline," and as a result the students only see them as disciplinarians and it irrevocably damages their ability to function in a counseling role.

Some principals have designated a discipline counselor. Often that role seems to have little to do with counseling. It is oftentimes a "judge" who listens carefully to the facts of each case and then metes out punishment. Sometimes principals will decree that such a role is rotated yearly through the counseling staff, but again, the counselor role is put on hold for a year for that assigned staffer, and it's often hard to regain the "counseling mental set" of the student who had previously dealt with someone as a disciplinarian/judge (e.g., one's podiatrist becoming one's cardiologist).

This is not to say that counselors should not be involved in "discipline." Discipline is too big a topic in education to be ignored by anyone involved in education. Choose to look upon discipline as self-control. Every student should have an A in self-control before they leave school. If they can't control themselves, know strategies for controlling themselves, and be able to execute those strategies as needed, then all the schooling in the world will be to no avail.

Every counselor *should* discuss self-control with each and every student referred to them. High-achieving students, ready for promotion or advancement to high school or college, should have discussed with their counselor their abilities to control anger, impulses, negative thoughts, attention, etc.—low-achieving students, likewise. Guidance classes dealing with self-control could be part of the curriculum.

Teachers, new and experienced, should be able to look upon counselors as sources of information and help in maintaining individual student and classroom management. The counseling office should be a place where teachers can explain complete situations in this area and expect to find solutions and comfort. New techniques such as eye pictures about the room (seem to encourage good behavior) or weighted vests (seem to calm upset students) could be shared and situations clarified.

Using counselors to assist parents who are having "discipline" problems at home, setting them up for two hours a week as a "control clinician" where parents can seek out discipline answers, is a way to solve immediate problems and enhance counselor image while explaining the counselor function. Counselors as self-control experts is a marvelous way for principals to involve counselors in the discipline question while maintaining their very important professional status. You will be ensuring that in your school students are being exposed to the important factors of control and resilience that will stand them in good stead throughout their lives. The foundation will be laid for future life situations that demand that these attributes be available to these young people.

Even in high school, it's never too late to start this type of training. The U.S. Army is proposing intense training in emotional resiliency, military officials say (*New York Times*, p. A1, Tuesday, August 18, 2009). Such training, it is hoped, will help ward off mental problems, depression, post-traumatic stress disorder, and suicide. A general stated in the article that he worried that our culture was not ready to accept this type of training for soldiers, perhaps it was too "touchy-feely." Yet one-fifth of the troops are experiencing the aforementioned mental problems, and our "culture" is not ready to offer them possible remedies of how to control these problems?

It might be possible to begin a "culture" readjustment if schools, through counseling programs, could begin to offer young students coping mechanisms for dealing with problems of resilience and control so they would feel more comfortable using such techniques as they grew older! What an opportunity to bend the "twig" in the right direction!

Motto: *Discipline is physical therapy for the mind. Neglecting to train students how to discipline themselves is not to educate them at all.*

Savvy Strategy 90: Total School Team Interim Evaluation

In Savvy Strategy 82 the importance of interim evaluations for counselors was discussed— reviewing yearly goals, seeing how far we had gone toward reaching them, etc. In addition, we have discussed how counseling is part of the school team. Now, it is being suggested that interim goal-achieving sessions be held in concert with all school areas; academic goals, counseling goals, athletic goals, physical goals, and more. At these meetings, representatives from each department would discuss achievements and barriers toward achievement, the goal of such meetings being how departments could work together to help one another.

For example, academic success depends to a large extent on the student's presence in the classroom. If absence is a major happening impeding such success, counseling should be mounting a strong attendance component to support the academic sector. If students are failing to keep counseling appointments because teachers will not excuse them from class, accommodations should be sought. If athletic commitments for practice and game participation can't be maintained because of academic failures or discipline infractions, steps should be taken by the academic and counseling departments to shore up these breaches so athletic commitments could be kept.

Educators must be given the opportunity to understand the various components that make up school life and learn to respect disciplines other than their own. Business leaders are constantly stressing the importance of coordinating the various elements in today's corporations. We as educators oftentimes operate in our own walled-off castles. As principals, the main leaders of the school corporation, we must try to grease the wheels of our various departments to effect a smooth-running togetherness—the hallmark of tomorrow. Remember, there is no "I" in *team*.

By attending scheduled meetings, the various professional disciplines get to meet together to address barriers to goal-achieving. Principals can help set the stage for colleagues to tap into one another's brain power, thereby getting to hear and hopefully respect the services of others. By having your counseling staff at these meetings and providing a *structured* opportunity for idea sharing, the stage is being set for successful goal achieving through cooperation.

Motto: *Help tear down those walls.*

Savvy Strategy 91: Report Successes, Share Success Strategies, Visualize Successes

Your program will have begun to achieve successes as you devote more of your attention to it. As a major proponent of good counseling efforts, mention them at faculty meetings and to others at district staff meetings. Do not hide your light under a bushel. Feel your program is successful, and visualize it as such. Think Donald Trump. He, more often than not, is recounting a successful happening in his life and refuting others who may be negating the same. Visualize your school as achieving all the goals that you have set for it. What would be different, how would it look? Visualize it down to the minutest detail and act as if this has happened or is just about to. What is being talked about here is your ability not to negate reality but to define reality by what you perceive and to perceive the success components of your program.

You have a group of counselors or a counselor who is/are focused on improving the program, who are tallying achievements and activities, who are working in concert with other staff members to support and improve their disciplines, who are aware of the existing culture and are moving to enhance and improve it. Take the time to note small successes (e.g., we've established two extra parent groups; career awareness programs are being conducted at the third-grade level; discipline referrals to the principal's office are down 10 percent) and report such happenings wherever it might be relevant.

By evidencing a success attitude and visualizing success happening, your staff will most likely emulate you and achieve the *energy* necessary for these accomplishments. The link between thinking it so and it happening or becoming so has been explored over and over.

The best-selling book *The Secret* by Rhonda Byrne highlights the process of deciding what you want, believing you can have it, believing you deserve it, visualizing already having it, and feeling grateful for it occurring as a major way of attaining your goals. Maxwell Maltz's famous psycho-cybernetics experiment of improved basketball shots by just visualizing successful layups has kept many of us in awe for years.

Give these programs a chance; think about the successful leaders you have known who have inspired you. Surely they, for the most part, were upbeat, they persevered, they always kept their "eye on the ball," they visualized success and achievement. And think about this effect on those about you. "One of the main functions of a good leader is to motivate," says Woody Sears in *Front Line Guide to Building High Performance Teams* (train, coach, discipline, counsel, motivate, and evaluate.). If your boss doesn't think you can achieve, it makes it doubly difficult to do so. Don't be a barrier to staff success—help them be winners, help yourself be the leader of the winning team. Have your counselors understand that you truly believe they can do the job and arrive at the agreed-upon goals. Building on your energy and your faith, they will make things happen.

Motto: *Visualizing is a strong first step toward achieving.*

Savvy Strategy 92: Associate with Positive Colleagues

Scientists believe that social networks not only can spread diseases (like common cold) but also influence many types of behavior both negative and positive that effect persons. The power of social networks has been examined over and over again. Influences are being noted in the physical manifestation of illness.

Of course, people are influenced by their friends, but how much so can be very surprising, as reported in a *New York Times* article (August 5, 2007, sect. 4, p. 1, "You, Your Friends, Your Friends of Friends," by Gina Kolata). Obesity can spread from friend to friend just like a virus (reported in the *New England Journal of Medicine,* August 27, 2007).

Social networks involve you, your family, your friends, your friends' friends, and your friends' friends' friends. The striking feature of these networks is that they amplify whatever effect they are propagating, as noted by Dr. Nicholas Christakis of Harvard Medical School. Dr. Christakis and his colleague, James H. Fowler, a political scientist at the University of California, San Diego, are now looking at depression and questioning whether it spreads from friend to friend.

You can name many instances in your own life where your friends' attitudes and opinions deeply affected your own. Think about the selection of your schools, places to live, vacations, and political beliefs. The above studies look at physical or bodily effects; mental effects seemingly are more readily discernable.

Negative colleagues can somehow make us feel down about things, less apt to take risks, less hopeful that goals can be achieved, less willing to try something new, less motivated to learn more about a particular topic, and more cynical about just about everything. However, they can also be more amusing, interesting, knowledgeable, and engaging than our more positive colleagues. Unfortunately, many times these negative colleagues can be members of your more senior staff who know more interesting anecdotes of the past and happenings of the present.

For your part, you may wish to:

1. Be aware of your negative comments.
2. Decide if negative comments far outweigh the positive ones.
3. Decide to have a "totally positive day" (maybe start with a half day).

Rejecting negativity can be a dilemma for an administrator wishing to try a new technique or trying to become an outstanding staff motivator or cheerleader of a discipline.

Do not alienate colleagues, do not set yourself apart, but try to identify those, who like yourself, are trying to energize, change, and redirect efforts. Protect yourself by not engaging in negativity or contributing to it. Try to find others who seem to feel as you do and network with them; you'll be doing yourself a favor. Negativity can wear you down and act as a barrier toward achieving what you desire.

Hear the counseling success stories; avoid hearing (if you can) the negative stories. Counter these with success stories of your own. Remember that you are projecting a circle of influence, and perhaps your words will turn some of those naysayers to ayesayers, and all will feel much better for it.

Motto: *Show me your friends and I'll show you who you are.*

Savvy Strategy 93: Have a Success Discussion

Jerry Porras, Stewart Emery, and Mark Thompson wrote, in *Success Built to Last*, that "extraordinary people, teams, and organizations are simply ordinary people doing extraordinary things that matter to them." It's important for success that what counselors are doing matters to them. Meeting for a success discussion can help to focus or refocus them in the right direction. Even if the discussion is with one or two counselors on your staff, ask questions such as (gleaned from Porras, Emery, and Thompson):

- Are you happy to be here everyday?
- Are you learning and growing professionally?
- Does your salary/level of responsibility match your aspirations?

- Can you list more positive than negative things about your job?
- Is what you're doing important to you?

Maybe it could be too difficult for counselors to discuss these questions openly with you, but you should convey to them that you want them to be successful and that their feeling successful can go a long way toward actually being successful. Counselors are usually in the position of reaching out to make others successful, but oftentimes the elements of personal success for them are overlooked or never addressed.

As a leader concerned with making each area of your school a success, it can be very valuable for you to take time to help your counselors think about what would have to be or have to happen to make them feel successful. By perhaps just touching on the aforementioned questions—not asking for verbal responses but posing the questions as thought-provoking ideas—you will help them to focus on and think about what would make them successful, and you'll have opened the door to this very important topic.

Listing what you've noted as program successes can set a very positive opening tone for this type of discussion. So many times we're addressing what needs to be done and how it's necessary to develop strategies to arrive at different goals. Remember to take time to look at what's already been achieved and examine the success feeling(s) that go along—or should go along—with these achievements.

A good leader helps staff identify successful elements in their lives and encourages their replication. "You've been successful in the past and you can be again." Sometimes it may happen that their jobs and achievements are not part of their personal definition of success for them. Such discussions, then, can be the catalyst for some staff members to see that perhaps it is time for them to move on to other venues where they can feel successful. How wonderful for you to be able to rekindle in them their personal success journey. For a good leader there can be no greater reward than developing individual staff members into successful, achieving professionals. Have the discussion—your team will be the stronger for it.

John Wooden (2005) defined success as "peace of mind which is a direct result of self-satisfaction in knowing you made the effort to become the best of which you are capable." What greater gift could you give your counseling staff members than the peace of mind we're all searching for today? What greater gift could you give your school than staff members striving to be the best of which they are capable? A win-win situation for all.

Motto: *Nail down success attitudes.*

Savvy Strategy 94: Get Them Off to a Great Start! (The First Day of School)

Every one of us has read articles and seen reports on TV and the Internet about the first school day. The classrooms are ready. The teachers are checking supplies. The bus drivers are interviewed. The principal is greeting parents and students at the door. The students are asked about their expectations, and parents are wondering about safety, achievement, and student success. Little if anything is ever mentioned about the counseling office or the counselors.

What a great time to ensure their utilization and visibility by developing some first-day-of-class strategies for counselors to bring to the attention of students, staff, and parents. As a principal you might wish counselors to prepare a blurb relevant to activities to have available for parents and/or students who stop by the main office of the school on some necessary first-day visit. Information should be available to students on that day as to how to access counseling services (this will most likely be redundant, but hearing about it again will help—hopefully—to solidify it).

The availability of counselors on the first school day as troubleshooters—helping students find classes, straightening out programs, and assisting parents who are having difficulty understanding some directions, can go a long way toward establishing them as *available* helpers from the get-go and as responsible and important school professionals. This is reaching-out time. Frequent contact, states Jack Carew in *The Mentor* (1998), is one of the strongest forms of bonding. Be there, be there, be there.

Getting this message to counseling staff is one of the most important things you can do. Oftentimes counselors may feel that "confidentiality" places a veil over them, and they remain in their offices—apart from the general fray. Confidentiality is important, but confidence keeping does not mean being invisible.

Having counselors seen as helpful, knowledgeable persons in the school surroundings by those they are there to help—students, teachers, parents—will go a long way toward getting these valuable staff members the attention and respect that can only enhance their efforts. Having these staff members visibly on board the first day of the school year should help contribute to their successful achievements throughout the term.

By providing attention to the needs of their clients and avoiding self-limiting types of behavior (e.g., "that's not exactly in my role description"), counselors can be seen as wholly committed to the overall success of the total school program—and this should begin on the very first day of school. So be sure all your departments are out there putting their best foot forward, being helpful, being seen, being there.

Motto: *Be there, be fair, CARE.*

Savvy Strategy 95: Not Always Mr. Nice Guy

Most every one of us wants to be liked and respected by our staff. We want to be able to listen, have patience, provide assistance, and compliment those in our employ. Unfortunately, there are times when compliments should not be forthcoming. The desire on the part of the school leader to be seen as nonthreatening—as someone who doesn't really take one to task but either leaves it to someone else or ignores the situation entirely—has led to what might be called "the under management epidemic" (Tulgan 2007).

Wanting to be nice is one thing, but not doing your job can hurt more than help. When you go "soft pedal" or ignore major errors or mistakes, when you refuse to act on information from assistant principals or head counselors that indicate certain counselors are not fulfilling their appropriate roles or are laying down on the job, arriving late, being unavailable during the school day, sharing confidences about students with others, talking down the school or the district, it can hurt rather than help your program.

There is something so secure and safe about being and having a strong leader; one who can manage a very delicate situation by either getting a staff member back on track or arranging for the dismissal of said person. Your job as principal is to be sure the information about a negative happening is true and then taking steps to correct the situation.

You may be able to pass it on to a subordinate to correct, but your leadership persona will be much more strongly enhanced if you take care of the tough situation yourself. Speaking directly to the offending or noncompliant staff member in a strong but controlled manner with all your facts in place might be the first step. Indicating your displeasure, asking for an explanation, making the decision on how to proceed—this is your role. This is what makes for a strong school, a successful school.

Schools should be warm and nurturing places for all who attend. Hopefully, as principal you can be that Mr. or Mrs. Nice Guy most of the time. However, it is important that all staff know that the helm is held by a strong leader who does not ignore (a favorite coping mechanism of leaders of late) difficult situations but acts quickly, intelligently, kindly, but surely to rectify them. By being sure from the beginning that counseling staff is clear on roles, tasks, and your expectations, you should be able to avoid many pitfalls. By having scheduled interim evaluation meetings, major failures can be headed off.

But when the icebergs appear, it's the captain who should take the helm and steer that ship out of harm's way. Ignoring the iceberg doesn't make it go away, and the "nice guy" can sink the ship.

Motto: *Sometimes NO is an answer.*

Savvy Strategy 96: Be Alert to How "Customers" Feel about Them

As you walk about your school, walk about the neighborhood, and shop in the markets in town, keep alert to comments relevant to counseling services. If you don't reside in the area, try to get outside the school at lunchtime or before you leave for home at the end of the day to perhaps walk in the park or pick up some groceries from the market. (If you don't feel safe doing this, you might ask yourself why children would feel differently and address this issue with city leaders). Listen for comments about the school and its services. In the school, observe the counseling office and review records. See if students, teachers, and parents are scheduled for appointments; if appointments are being kept; if clients are arriving on time; if clients are kept waiting.

Inform counselors that you are concerned about the image of school services as well as about the delivery and effectiveness of same. Discuss with them the value of feedback from "customers" and how this might be done in an informed and nonthreatening way. Questions to ask might include:

1. Do students know why they are seeing you?
2. Have you ever asked a student to evaluate the service he or she has received from the counseling office, or from you in particular?
3. Do you self-evaluate? After a particular teacher guidance session, do you ask yourself: What did that teacher get from my efforts to help her with her classroom management problems?
4. What might students tell their friends regarding your helpfulness and the effectiveness of your services?
5. If you were a student in this school, would you seek help from you?
6. If a student, teacher, or parent doesn't show up for an appointment, do you make a follow-up call, send an e-mail, write a note?
7. Do you feel you need more training, research, or support in order to provide the appropriate training for students?

The above questions and others you might feel more on target for your particular situation can serve as springboards toward assessing a service image and toward developing techniques and procedures for changing a negative image into a more positive and effective one. *Do not* neglect to talk about image. Of course, effective image change does not happen overnight, but word can spread quickly that counselors are evidencing major concerns about the state of their helpfulness—concern bordering on caring—and that's a positive in anyone's book.

A good service can be hindered by a poor reputation or negative aura just as a good picture can be diminished by a crumbling frame. The loveliest diamond is thrillingly enhanced in a shining setting. Politicians strive mightily to place the proper "spin" on all their actions. A good school leader makes every effort to have all departments deliver their best services. Why not be sure that they are being seen in their best light? Why not be sure that all staff members are aware of the importance of image, and that it is important to you?

Motto: *Have your fingers on the pulse of the situation.*

Savvy Strategy 97: What about Crisis Plans, Teams, Situations

Today, most every school and every district is mandated to have a crisis plan. How will the school react in terms of a crisis situation (e.g., threatened suicide, suicide, shooter, terrorist takeover, illness, fire, etc.)? Depending on the district, the crisis plan can be highly detailed or rather sketchy. Counselors are most usually involved in the plan to some extent. At times they are often designated as the crisis team leader (most crisis plans call for the development of a crisis team). The plans usually have three main areas of concentration: crisis prevention, crisis occurrence, and crisis follow-up.

Time is often spent on developing the plan: assigning personnel to various tasks, being sure the plan is in compliance with home district guidelines, and writing up the plan and forwarding it on to the district office. Hopefully, there will be in that plan the listing of a schedule of specific times when that plan will be reviewed and personnel realerted to their various duties.

Oftentimes plans are developed, counselors are designated as crisis team leaders, and then—nothing. No one really knows what to do and looks to you, the principal, to guide them. Certain plans call for highly specific activities to take place in order to prevent possible death and to ensure every chance of survival.

Some schools may wish to discuss certain suggestions for teacher/student behaviors if taken hostage:

- Being compliant
- Being polite
- Not joking around, etc. (see Martin Carruthers, Soulwork Systematic Solution, soulwork@gmx.de).

Some schools have included certain suggestions for managers' behaviors if taken hostage:

- Do whatever the armed hostage taker wants.
- Be especially courteous and compliant during the first ten minutes.
- Speak only when spoken to and do not offer jokes, sarcasm, or philosophy.
- Show passive compliance, act relaxed, and sit down if allowed.
- Don't turn your back and reach down unless so instructed.
- Try to maintain eye contact without staring.
- Weigh any chance to escape carefully.
- Be patient and trust negotiators (systematic solutions and relationships management).

These suggestions might save lives. Just hearing them once, or not hearing them at all, does little or no good at all. As leaders of crisis teams, counselors must be able to have the team practice and review all steps geared toward saving lives. Regularly scheduled meetings are important. Counselors should be able to schedule meetings for training (with "stars" [see Savvy Strategy 38]) in this field (e.g., Larry Chavez, Sacramento, California, police department, 916-354-2265; Jeffrey Daniels, assistant professor, Department of Education and Psychology, Indiana University, Bloomington, Indiana, 812-856-8304; Dr. Paul M. Violhes, president, Risk Control Strategies, Los Angeles, California; Dr. Lenore Terr, psychiatrist, San Francisco, California).

Being prepared in crisis situations has often been linked to the counseling staff's role. Providing them with the time to carry out this role effectively and with the proper training is a major consideration for the principal. Having backup for counselors (as mentioned in Savvy Strategy 22) when they are called to give unscheduled sessions to traumatized students and perhaps staff members might be another way to quickly smooth over a crisis and underscore the importance of everyday counseling services.

As mentioned before, a cohort of retired counselors kept at the ready by an ever-prepared principal could keep programs running effectively and maintain a quality school life while the regular counseling staff acts as crisis team leaders. Having a listing of such support personnel readily available will greatly assist the school and you, the school's principal. Forewarned is forearmed. Remember: Student safety and security is everyone's main concern.

Motto: *Crises do occur—the best defense is to be prepared.*

Savvy Strategy 98: Get Out There

Just as you would visit classrooms, the lunchroom, the gym, the yard, the boiler room, the computer lab, and the various street corners around the school where the different cliques gather—visit the counselor's office and the counseling suite (the outer office where records are kept and secretaries make appointments). Observe the conditions and the happenings—ask yourself if you would feel comfortable going to that setting. If answer is no—what might make it more comfortable, and how might you be able to effect that change? Ask to sit in on a group session (not counseling) with parents, with students, and with staff and *wait* to receive an invitation. If no invitation is advanced, don't go, but you can question why. Oftentimes just asking to attend can shape up a session.

Check to see if records are kept securely and who has access to them. With so many technological advances the question of student privacy, accuracy of records, and security of information is a very important one and should not be approached in a cavalier manner or left to chance.

If the school has onsite security personnel, they should be alerted to the fact of the importance of the safety and security of the school records and counseling records and be alerted to whatever steps must be taken to ensure the same. Take note of the area provided for waiting and how clients are made aware of the fact that the counselor might have had to cancel an appointment or is attending to another matter.

In selected schools, especially at the elementary level, there is often no outside suite. In that case, the counselor's schedule should be placed on the door—at a low-enough level for elementary students to read clearly. A secure compartment or box should be attached to the door so students or staff or parents may leave notes for the counselor if they should so desire. Every effort should be maintained to assist student(s) if an emergency occurs. In the counselor's absence they might be referred to the principal or assistant principal (at the elementary level).

At the middle or high school level, more staff is usually available—but a student or other school personnel or parents should *always* be able to reach counseling personnel in an emergency or be aware of someone else who would be available to them. This emergency information should be readily made known to inquirers by being clearly noted on the counselor's office door (e.g., "I have been called away. In emergency contact *name, location* immediately.") Counselors should always have checked to be sure that an emergency referral person is readily available on that particular date.

By "getting out there," you, as principal, can make certain that these measures are in place and also, lacking an emergency situation, that normal operating procedures (e.g., individual counseling sessions, group counseling sessions, record maintenance time) are also proceeding as scheduled. You are the boss, the leader, the keeper of the flame, so to speak. Check to see, in person, that the flame is burning brightly—do not rely only on reports of subordinates. Staff will soon become aware of your hands-on involvement procedures and act accordingly.

Motto: *The buck stops here.*

Savvy Strategy 99: Maintain Focus/Ask the Right Questions

Remember what you want for your school and check frequently to see if your staff is moving in that direction. This checking can be done by reviewing reports, observing procedures, examining various evaluation measurements instruments, talking with consumers, and walking about your school, tuning in to its own special life beat.

A district superintendent in New York City once stated, "I can go into a school and in 15 minutes of walking about I can tell whether it's doing well or doing poorly." Other principals say similar things, which leads one to believe that perhaps there is a certain life beat that emanates from a school and is discernable to certain educators.

However you feel, you can always learn quite a bit by asking the right questions. If your overall school goal is to improve the reading scores in your school and you've geared all staff into that goal, then ask your counselors, "What did you do to improve the reading scores—this week—this month—today?"

If your goal is to decrease the number of students being referred to the school nurse for obesity reasons, you may wish to ask counselors, "What procedures did you engage in—this week—this month—today—geared toward decreasing obesity?"

Such questions help staff to maintain focus on overall goals while awareness of this modus operandi of yours keeps them alert to the fact that their actions—daily, weekly, etc.—are important and being monitored. How often have we as educators been made aware of the fact that unchecked homework often becomes undone homework? When you, the school leader, repeatedly question staff members regarding activities toward reaching their goal, the importance of that goal is underscored.

The secret, of course, is in how the questions are asked.

1. Is there a sincere interest in the answer, and is the interest clearly projected by the questioner? Or is this an "I gotcha" type situation—where the questioner projects a hope of catching the staff member "off guard"?
2. Is there a manifestation of gratitude or delight on the part of the questioner (e.g., "That sounds great," "I'm so glad that's working out," "What a great idea. I'd like to share it with my colleagues," or "Good work, I think we're going to make it.")?
3. Ask if there is some way you can help, some barrier you can be of assistance in getting removed—and then be sure to try to provide this assistance.
4. Stand still and look at the counselor when you're asking questions like this—showing concern and interest is just that. Standing still and *showing* interest.

Questions can be doors to greater communication, respect, and achievement. They can be of a personal nature, but the setting for such should usually be private. Questions are sometimes perfunctory—part of the social ballet of life. Don't expect to get too much from that type of question (e.g., "How are you?"). The questions, the special questions we are noting here, have to do with substance, sincerity, and a striving for success. If you can link these factors together, your questions will form a firm foundation for the ongoing performance of your programs.

Counselors, for example, can be strongly linked to reading achievement through bibliotherapy sessions with counselees and instructional guidance groups for parents that show them how, when, and why to read to their young children. We can make the education dream happen by all of us working together. The question is, "When will we?"

Motto: *Help them keep their eye on the ball.*

Savvy Strategy 100: Be a Great Manager and Coach

At the fiftieth anniversary of the LA Dodgers' move to Los Angeles, celebrated at the Hollywood Bowl on July 3, 2008, Tommy Lasorda, the legendary manager of the Dodgers, told the story of the year his team had lost seven games in a row and then turned that losing streak around and went on to win the pennant. After that seventh game loss, the famous manager told his wife one night—he spoke to his very downcast team in their locker room before game eight—that he tried his best to encourage them, listing all their strengths, their abilities, the love of their fans, etc.

Finally, reaching deep into his lexicon of stories, he told them his memory of the 1927 Yankees team who had lost nine games in a row—then turned things around and went on to win the pennant. Well, the fired-up team took to the field with a new gusto and began a winning streak that took them all the way to the pennant! "Wow!" commented Mrs. Lasorda, "how did you remember that?" "I didn't," responded the coach. "I was born that year. I made it up."

Everyone in the huge Hollywood Bowl loved the story, and all realized the importance of that outside motivator, that person who helps you, gives you that extra boost, pushes the right buttons, and helps you achieve the success you desire.

This is your job as chief school manager. Not fabricating stories (well, maybe a little stretch or more positive spin), but encouraging those who you know are capable to push on when they might feel that all is lost. Bring to their attention areas of assistance of which they might not be aware (e.g., California Assembly Bill 1802 provides extra funding to compensate counselors for time spent working with students outside the regular work day). This would include conferring with parents and students to give them a realistic picture of where they stand and what they can do to improve. Information of this type shows legislative validation for the importance of counselors' efforts and should help to strengthen counselors' own perceptions of the value of their efforts.

Part of your job, besides motivating to success but closely aligned with it, is to coach, to guide, to help staff succeed. There is a famous exercise underscoring the value of coaching:

1. Place a basket on the floor.
2. Give the coachee some wadded-up paper.
3. Ask them to pitch the wad into the basket from about seven feet away.
4. Blindfold them.
5. Spin them around so they are not facing (and don't know) where the basket is.

6. Ask them to pitch the wad into the basket.
7. When they miss, say you will help them—if they follow directions.
8. Guide them verbally (e.g., turn around, pitch lower, pitch further to left, pitch a little further, etc.).
9. With coaching, they will come much closer and probably score! And you've demonstrated the importance of getting help.

Unfortunately, many times coaching might be seen as criticism. And everyone usually hates criticism. Darren Gurney, a high school teacher in New Rochelle, New York, and also a high school and college baseball team coach (*New York Times* Business, August 29, 2009, p. B6, "For Best Results, Take the Sting Out of Criticism," by Alina Tugend), feels the best way to critique is to ask players to analyze what happened and how they might have done better. Help counselors do this when goals haven't been reached.

We have a built-in mechanism for trying to protect ourselves and a built-in mechanism for responding positively when positive things are done for us. (Although sometimes this one needs frequent priming with trust oil!) Giving critiques and feedback, complimenting well-done tasks, involving, motivating, supporting, and showing pride in achievements—expecting the best and not settling for average, that's your job. Counselors as a group are concerned with students for the long run. By becoming actively involved with counselors as their leader, administrators are professing their dedication to the long run.

Motto: *Thanks coach. I couldn't do it without you.*

Savvy Strategy 101: *Know* You Can Do It and Do It Now

Believing in the strength and value of your leadership and your ability to achieve your goals will become the hallmark of your success. You will be the one placing the long-hidden diamond of counseling and guidance in the beautiful Tiffany setting so that it can truly shine in a stunning brilliance. (Well, perhaps a little flowery, but meaningful.)

Be the principal who gives unsolicited praise to his guidance and counseling staff. Engage in discussions that say how important it is to have counseling personnel available for students. Comment on the need for counselors, the value of counseling, and the changing role for counselors.

This is territory that is wide open for your assistance. Proper support, placement, and encouragement for today's students are critical. Counselors can give this to students, and you can help them do it. Your qualities of leadership should make staff want to commit to easily definable and demonstrated goals.

As a leader you should be able to praise with honesty and genuineness. You should be able to foster staff support of each other so that each can recognize the effectiveness of working together under your direction and leadership while eschewing internal carping and criticism.

A Gates Foundation–funded study of over forty thousand teachers reported in *Time* magazine's Briefing Section on March 15, 2010, found that while at least 45 percent of those surveyed highlighted the importance of good salaries "as essential to retaining good instructors . . .," some "68% cited 'the importance' of quality leadership." You're building a winning team; try to build it on openness, knowledge, mutual respect, and support. Avoid, if you can, threats and penalties, but do not be afraid to exercise them if absolutely necessary. Demonstrate the high quality of leadership that all in education are hungering for.

And don't procrastinate. Time is a commodity that is constantly being used up. The motto "Just do it" can't be faulted. If tough decisions have to be made, it's you who must make them—delaying helps sometimes—but usually not. But be swift to support, praise, coach, and motivate, also.

You are the leader, the boss—you can do it. Do it now.

Motto: *As Nike says, "Just do it."*

The Super Principal's Checklist

1. Do you get involved in counselor selection from the very beginning?
2. Do you include counselor and counselor programs in staff meeting planning and agendas?
3. Do you include the counselor in advisory groups?
4. Do you include counselors in your district meetings?
5. Are you fully aware of and involved in the development of counselor goals and objectives for your school?
6. Do you provide for opportunities for counselor staff development?
7. Does your budget planning provide for adequate housing, compensation, supplies, and professional programs for counselors?
8. Do you have at least a cursory knowledge of counseling techniques and procedures?
9. Do you have a formal and ongoing evaluation program for counseling?
10. Do you make revisions and/or adjustments to the program in light of evaluation results?
11. Do you see yourself as one who coaches your counselors to be successful?
12. Do you feel counseling programs are as important as straight academic programs?

Answering yes to all twelve questions indicates you're a super principal!

Selected Bibliography for Principals

Anderson, Redia, and Lenora Billings-Harris. *Trailblazers: How Top Business Leaders Are Accelerating Results through Inclusion and Diversity*. John Wiley & Son: Hoboken, NJ, 2010.
Bryant, Annie. *Lake Rescue* (Beacon Street Girls #6). North Richland Hills, TX: Aladdin Publishing/Simon & Schuster, 2008.
Byrne, Rhonda. *The Secret*. New York: Simon & Schuster, 2006.
Carew, Jack. *The Mentor*. New York: Donald J. Fine Books (Penguin Group), 1999.
Crowley, Karen. *New York Times*, Sports Sunday section, September 30, 2007.
Goleman, Daniel. *Emotional Intelligence: Why It Can Matter More Than I.Q.* New York: Bantam Press, 2000.
Holmes, J. H., and R. H. Rahe, "The Social Readjustment Rating Scale." *Journal of Psychosomatic Research* (1967): 213–18, esp. 216.
Kalish, Nancy. *Prevention Magazine* (re: Brainpower) (May 9, 2007), quoted by Paul Brown, *New York Times*, Media and Advertising section, October 6, 2007.
Klass, Perri. "Making Room for Miss Manners." *New York Times* Health section (January 12, 2009).
Krames, Jeffrey. *Jack Welch on Leadership*. New York: McGraw Hill, 2005.
Maltz, Maxwell. *Psycho-Cybernetics*. New York: Simon & Schuster, 1989.
Martin, Judith. *Miss Manners' Guide to Rearing Perfect Children*. New York: W.W. Norton & Co., 2005.
National Center for Clinical Infant Programs Report, 1992.
New York Times. "Emotional Resiliency for Military" (August 18, 2009): A1.
Parker, Pope. *New York Times* Health section (October 14, 2008): D5.
Porras, Jerry, Stewart Emery, and Mark Thompson. *Success Built to Last*. Upper Saddle River, NJ: Wharton School Publication, 2006.

Putzier, John, and David Baker. *The Everything HR Kit: A Complete Guide to Attracting, Retaining, and Motivating High-Performance Employees.* New York: AMACOM, 2011.

Sears, Woodrow Dr. *Front Line Guide to Building High Performance Teams.* Amherst, MA: HRD Press, 2007.

Sills, Judith. "Jump for Job Joy." *Psychology Today,* September 1, 2007.

Terr, Lenore, MD. *Unchained Memories.* New York: HarperCollins, 1994.

Tugend, Alina. "For Best Results Take the Sting Out of Criticism." *New York Times* Business section (August 28, 2009).

Tulgan, Bruce. *It's Okay to Be the Boss.* New York: HarperCollins, 2007.

UCLA Center for Mental Health in the Schools. *Addressing Barriers to Learning* 12, 1 (Winter 2007). Department of Psychology, UCLA, Los Angeles, CA.

Wall Street Journal (re: Kathy Morgan, All Hallows High School counselor story) (April 1999).

Welsh, Jack. *Jack.* New York: Grand Central Publishing, 2001.

Wooden, John. *Wooden on Leadership.* New York: McGraw Hill, 2005.

Appendix A: Sample Grid

Appendix A: Sample Grid

Time	Monday	Tuesday	Wednesday	Thursday	Friday
8:00–9:00	Office Student Interviews	Office Counseling Interviews	Office Student Interviews	Office Interviews	Office Interviews
9:00–10:00	Parent Workshops Auditorium	Test Preparation Room 410	Parent Workshops Auditorium	Test Preparation Room 412	Individual Parent Meetings Office
10:00–11:00	Classroom Observation Room ____	Classroom Observation Room ____	Record Prep & Review Office	Record Prep & Review Office	Telephone Contacts with Agencies Office
12:00–1:00	Lunch Meeting with Teachers Room ____	Group Counseling Room ____	Group Counseling Room ____	Group Counseling Room ____	Group Counseling Room ____
1:00–2:00	Office Interviews	Lunch Interviews	Lunch Interviews	Lunch Interviews	Lunch Interviews
2:00–3:00	Office Interviews	Office Interviews	Office Interviews	Office Interviews	Office Interviews
3:00–4:00	Home Visitations	Records and ____ Calls Office	Records and ____ Calls Office	Parent Meetings Room ____	Parent Meetings Room ____
4:00–5:00	School Meetings Location ____	Parent Group Location ____	Parent Group Location ____	Seminar Session Location ____	Seminar Session Location ____

Motto: *Let them know where you go.*

Appendix B: Log of Guidance Services

_____ **Unified School District**
Report of Fiscal and Community Involvements

Counselor services in the _____ Unified School District are directed toward assisting students in the achievement of their maximum potential. In addition, we are ever vigilant regarding areas of special concern and interest occurring at specific times. As a result, we have given special focus at this time to the areas of finance and community involvement.

It is our hope that the following chart will convey the major results of our efforts in these two areas only.

(Note: These two areas selected for presentation make up only a part of the counselor's multiactivity-oriented year.)

Fiscal Involvements

College scholarships obtained for students

\# _____ $ _____

Community college scholarships

\# _____ $ _____

ADA returned to district as a result of counseling absentees

Number of students involved _____

Cash value $ _____

Intern services secured

Number of interns   _____

Cash value (based on % of teacher time) $ _____

Decrease in school vandalism costs as a result of counseling

Number of students in program _____

Cash value $ _____

Work experience provided

Number of students   _____

Cash value $ _____

Employment secured for graduates

Number of students   _____

Cash value $ _____

Community Involvements

Number of parents contacted regarding academic achievement of students

_____

Number of telephone calls made to parents regarding:

    achievement   _____
    behavior   _____
    attendance   _____
    other   _____

Number of contacts with community agencies for referrals

_____

Number of appearances at PTA meetings

_____

Number of speeches made at community meetings (PTA included)

_____

Number of letters sent to parents

_____

Number of notices sent to community

_____

Number of bulletins developed for community

_____

Part-time employment for students
Number of students   _____
Cash value $_____

Grants obtained
Number of grants   _____
Cash value $_____

Substituting for absent teachers
Number   _____
Cash value $_____

Funds for items obtained through counselor's personal contacts
Number of items   _____
Cash value $_____

Number of speeches made at community meetings (PTA included)

_____

Number of letters sent to parents

_____

Number of notices sent to community

_____

Number of bulletins developed for community

_____

Number of employers contacted for potential students

_____

Appendix C: Numerical Report on Counseling Activities

Month	Students Seen (Purposes)								Parents Seen		Staff Seen		Additional				
	Academic	Career	Personal	Crisis	Attendance	Discipline	Group Counseling Sessions		Individual	Groups	Individual	Groups	Inservice Sessions Given	Referrals Out	Community Presentations	Meetings Attended	Courses Taken	Telephone Calls
Week I																		
Week II																		
Week III																		
Week IV																		
Week V																		
Totals																		

Appendix D: Fog Index*

To work out your own Fog Index, test any one hundred words that you write: a report, speech, or article. Divide that one hundred by the number of sentences used. Then note how many complex words you use for every one hundred you write (a complex word is one with three syllables or more—not counting words with capital letters). Take four-tenths of the total and that is your Fog Index.

Example: If you average twenty words to a sentence, and ten complex words in one hundred: add 20 and 10 and you get 30. Calculate four-tenths of 30, which is 12. Your Fog Index is 12. For comparison, the *Reader's Digest* has a Fog Index of between 8 and 9; *Time* is 11. If the score is over 13, it is hard to read.

The Learning Revolution, by Gordon Dryden and Jeannette Vos, Jalmar Press, Carson, California, 1987.

---

*Joseph Peart and Jim R. McNamara, in *The New Zealand Handbook of Public Relations*, published by Mills Publications, Lower Hutt, New Zealand, 1987, attribute the invention of the Fog Index to Robert Gunning, an American businessman.

Appendix E: Adam and Alice's Magic Tips for Talking to Adults

Appendix E: Adam and Alice's Magic Tips for Talking to Adults

OFFICE OF THE LOS ANGELES COUNTY
SUPERINTENDENT OF SCHOOLS

An Official Publication
**Office of the Los Angeles County
Superintendent of Schools**
9300 E. Imperial Highway
Downey, CA 90242

Los Angeles County Board of Education
Dr. Daniel L. Towler, *President*
Dr. Earl V. Pullias, *Vice-President*
Lawrence J. Kaplan, D.D.S.
Ms. Louise H. Marsh
Ricardo J. Olivarez
Mrs. Angie Papadakis
Mrs. Kathryn Vanderhook

Permission to include in this document
was given on 10/24/03.

Frank Kwan, director
Communications Department
Los Angeles County Office of Education

Shari Kim Gale, legal staff
Los Angeles County Office of Education

Appendix E: Adam and Alice's Magic Tips for Talking to Adults ~ 151

Written by A. A. SESNO

Illustrated by V. WATANABE

Suggested by the
Los Angeles County
Mental Health Committee of the
International Year of the Child

152 ~ Appendix E: Adam and Alice's Magic Tips for Talking to Adults

Appendix E: Adam and Alice's Magic Tips for Talking to Adults — 153

Sad times can happen when we have to move away from the town we love, and friends we like so much.

It's also a sad and scary time when a report card is too bad to take home or when mother

has to go to the hospital or father has to leave home for business.

4

Or no one asks us to a birthday party, or the dog gets lost or we have bad dreams...

Or people get angry at us and no one seems to care and we feel very sad.

5

Appendix E: Adam and Alice's Magic Tips for Talking to Adults

Or we are afraid—
of school,
of being alone
of other kids,
of grown-ups.

All these things have happened to us and we are still here, and we feel pretty good!

So, if these things happen to you, remember, being unhappy happens to everyone. Yes everyone! Your parents, your teacher, even that super smart kid in your class— EVERYONE!

There is nothing wrong with being unhappy.

It just doesn't feel good. The important thing to know is how to handle being unhappy.

There are a few things you can do to start being happy again and the main thing we have found that helps is... TALKING THINGS OVER WITH SOMEONE!

Appendix E: Adam and Alice's Magic Tips for Talking to Adults   155

It usually helps to talk with a grown-up person you know and like. (they call themselves adults!)

First and most important are the people in your family. Your Mom, Dad, older brothers, sisters, Grandma or Grandpa. Teachers, counselors or the school nurse can help too.

We have found (and we have tried them all) most of them are glad to help when they really hear us.

But sometimes, we don't ask because—

We are afraid they will yell at us or blame us.

Or sometimes, we don't know the right words to say or the adults seem too busy, or won't listen.

Well, all these things have stopped us from talking to adults (grown-ups), too when we were unhappy.

156 ~ Appendix E: Adam and Alice's Magic Tips for Talking to Adults

But then we stayed unhappy, and that was no fun.

We knew the way to feeling better was to talk, so we began to think of ways of getting through (talking) to adults.

It took some trying, but after a while some things began to work like magic!
We want to share these magic tips with you.

MAGIC TIPS
First and most important - Pick a good time and place to talk.
Don't try to talk to adults when they are rushing to work or talking on the telephone, or seem very sad or angry themselves.

A good time to talk could be: When you are alone at home with them, or riding in a car with them, and they seem happy. Or it's a sunny day and it's quiet at home.

Appendix E: Adam and Alice's Magic Tips for Talking to Adults   157

Of course if it's very very important, tell them right away!

Second, when it's really hard to get their attention - say, "I have something important to tell you that I can't tell anyone else."

Third, touch them - very softly. Grown-ups don't mind being touched. In fact they like it - So do we! A soft touch is another way of saying "I like you-please listen to me."

Sometimes PRACTICING what to say first helps.

Say, "Please listen...."
"I'm scared....."
"I wasn't invited....."
"I got a bad mark....."
"I don't know how to...."
"Where is daddy...when is he coming home?"
"Will Mommy come back from the hospital?"
"I need your help....."
"What can I do about....."

158 ~ Appendix E: Adam and Alice's Magic Tips for Talking to Adults

And when you are finished talking, LISTEN. Sometimes it's not so easy to listen, but — if you want to be listened to — then you must listen.

Practice listening to:
Your sister or brother
The radio
T.V. (with your eyes closed)
The Teachers (they'll love it)
Your friends

LISTENING HELPS!

When you are listening or talking LOOK at the person. It will make you feel closer to them and them feel closer to you.

And don't forget to tell them "Thank You" or that you like it when they help you. Everyone likes to be thanked.

Appendix E: Adam and Alice's Magic Tips for Talking to Adults ~ 159

So remember...

OUR TIPS FOR TALKING TO ADULTS

1. Pick the Right Time
2. Get their Attention
3. Touch Softly
4. Go Close and Talk Softly
5. Practice what you want to Say
6. Listen to the Answers
7. Look at the Person
8. Say "Thank You"

(Maybe you can add some of your ideas to this list.)

_____

_____

Until the next time
Keep trying
Keep talking
Keep listening
and be happy

16

If you want to-write to:

Your name
Your address
Your town

COUNSELOR'S NAME
SCHOOL ADDRESS

and tell us your tips for talking to Adults.

Or tell us some of your problems. We'd love to hear from you, and we'll try to answer every letter!

So, when you write to us don't forget to include your name and your address.

17

About the Author

Alice Healy Sesno received her PhD from Fordham University, New York, in educational psychology, tests, and measurements. She has served as a teacher, counselor/coordinator, and administrator in the New York City School system and the New York State Department of Education in Albany, New York.

Dr. Sesno has also served as the Illinois director of Law-Focused Education and the assistant director for the Law in America Society Foundation. As consultant-in-charge for the Los Angeles County Office of Education, Dr. Sesno was responsible for the areas of school guidance, counseling, and evaluation. She has served on the faculties of Fordham University in New York and Loyola Marymount University in California.

Dr. Sesno has also been a member of the executive committee of the Inter-Agency Council for Child Abuse and Neglect in Los Angeles and served as chair of the Los Angeles County Task Force on Self-Esteem and Personal and Social Responsibility. For those efforts, she received a Special Recognition Award from the Los Angeles County Board of Supervisors, as well as the California Association for Counseling and Development and the Los Angeles County Pupil Personnel Directors.

Dr. Sesno has authored and coauthored many educational publications over the years, including the California State Department of Education's document, *Suicide Prevention in California Public Schools*. She has guest lectured and presented at a multiplicity of educational conferences and universities across the United States. Her most recent book, *97 Savvy Secrets for Protecting Self and School: A Guide for Teachers and Administrators*, was published by Corwin Press, Inc.

Most recently, Dr. Sesno has been serving as field supervisor for the Urban Intern Education Program at the University of California, Los Angeles.

www.ingramcontent.com/pod-product-compliance
Lightning Source LLC
Chambersburg PA
CBHW030319020526
44117CB00029B/181